Beauty *within* Weddings

BHUPINDER KUMAR PALL

First Published in April 2023

ISBN: 978-93-5741-543-9

BLUEROSE PUBLISHERS

www.BlueRoseONE.com

info@bluerosepublishers.com

+91 8882 898 898

Typographic Design:

Pooja Sharma

Distributed by: BlueRose, Amazon, Flipkart

Beauty Within Weddings

Fabulous Signature Indian Weddings

"About 30,000 weddings taking place per day, on average, in India. 900,000 weddings a month, more than 10 million per year."

"A dream book filled with beauty of inherited culture, traditions, customs, fun and frolic"

Organizing and Arranging Weddings is my passion. A firebrand wedding tycoon of India

www.kudmai.com

Bhupinder Kumar Pall

Author

To be Writer and Author is a beautiful Life

JOSHUA IRSHAD

Co-author

EDITING, SELF PUBLISHING & BOOK DESIGNING

(Also writer/author of 3 books)

Introduction

India is a land of diversities. This diversity is also visible in the spheres of religion, food, language, dresses, etc. The major religions of India are Hinduism (majority religion), Islam (largest minority religion), Sikhism, Christianity, Buddhism, Jainism, Zoroastrianism, Judaism and the Bahai Faith.

About 30,000 weddings taking place adayin India. Over

900,000 weddings are held per month, more than 10 million per year.

In this this book both authors Bhupinder and Joshua explore regional weddings of India, their rich blended cultural heritage, traditions and series of wedding rituals. Bhupinder is firebrand weddings planner, organizer. He has to his credit several of weddings successfully organized in India and abroad.

Officially there are 122 languages but 22 languages in the Eighth Schedule of the constitution give cultural pockets like Assamese, Gujarati, Konkani, Maithili, Manipuri, Oriya, Tamil, Telugu, etc.

Hindu weddings are vibrant, intricately planned, culture-rich festivities full of celebration and traditionally oriented. While the very essence of a Hindu wedding ceremony is the physical, spiritual, and emotional union of two people; it's also about the coming together of two families through wedding religious rituals and celebration.

Nevertheless, there are a few key rituals common in Hindu weddings Kanyadaan (handover daughter to groom), Panigrahana, and Saptapadi; these are respectively, traditionally gifting away of daughter by the father, voluntarily holding hand near the fire to signify impending union, and taking seven steps or circles before fire with each step or circle including a set of mutual vows.

The host of a culture that has been prevalent for a long time, India is perhaps one of the most diverse countries in the world. From the attire worn by the people belonging to different communities to the languages spoken and even in the food habits, the country both reflects its amazing diversity and varied heritage. India is considered the birthplace of some of the world's major religions: Buddhism, Hinduism, Jainism and Sikhism. Today, other religions such as Muslim and Christianity have worked their way into the population as well, though Hinduism remains the most popular.

India not only possesses racial diversity but also linguistic diversity. Some of the prominent language recognized by the constitution includes, Assamese, Bengali, Guajarati, Hindi, Kannad, Kashmiri, and Malayalam, Marathi, Punjabi, Sanskrit, Sindhi, Terrill, Telegu and Urdu.

Bhupinderholds , with pride, getting organized married thousands of young and old souls globally and nationally with great success. This book is both Bhupinder and Joshua dream book, which they want to present to global community to read and enjoy the rich treasure of beauty within weddings happen in India. Both found that Indian weddings have till now preserved the culture, traditions and customs, which otherwise would have been vanished and invaded by modernization and latest trend of Indian weddings.

Author's Page

Joshua and Bhupinder both decided to write this book "Beauty within Wedding." Both sit together and ponder over with strenuously determination to publish this book as they know each other talents and wants to present it in the shape of a book to global community as no one can escape from needed parasite of wedding.

Bhupinder is co-founder of www.kudmai.com. His journey triggered with largest corporate house of India and was designated the marketing section. He is managing director of helping life, India. But journey for Joshua influenced by his faithful dedicated missionaries parents. His field was humanitarian, relief, sustainable development, shelter, rehabilitation, social development, food insecurity and enhancing literacy where he worked internationally, also in collaborating with United Nations' agencies.

Since Bhupinder had great passion, vision, and mission how to be arrange, organized and manage weddings. And that resulted in launching website: www.kudmai.com, which was his dream project. Marketing, organizing wedding nationally and globally is his inseparable passion, difficult to part away this passion made him to remain in his country of origin India and author books on this tasteful subject of Indian diverse wedding along with Joshua.

Bhupinder grand-parents worked, resides in UK, likewise his parents reside in USA, but his love for weddings made him to stay where his roots are. He never bother for craze of settling down in these country of great reputation and better life. Never in life he looked towards these affluent country but great passion for world of wedding and finally "beauty within wedding" his long dream to unfold before the readers about the amazing world of culture, traditions, customs, modern, regional weddings closely connected with nuptials happening in large scale in India. Different styles, ceremonies, rituals and practice blended with weddings and the beauty inherited in weddings ceremonies he has personally witnessed which he himself organized are worth reading and leafing through this book can enlighten the reader about hidden treasure within beauty of Indian marriages.

Bhupinder never looked back deviating from this wonder filled subject of weddings ceremonies, rituals, practices filled with fun and frolics. The journey of his passion for weddings will be filled with enriched knowledge for readers to go in depth to know the splendid secrets hidden within cultural, traditional weddings especially indian regional weddings.

Bhupinder journeyed thousand miles in connection with organizing weddings, careful to meet still unmarried couple and preparing themwith personal touchof advice to have blessed long life for nuptial which he organized himself. "Weddings are made in heaven", but he is great spirit that made the " wedding heaven on earth" as a great success. He strongly believe in personal approach, extended wedding counseling, advise, transparency for couple he is going to get tie the knot of eternal life spending togather as blessed couple with flourishing life overflowing with joy, peace and everlasting companionship. Indian pre weddings system is inherited with so many cultural barriers, which cannot be ignored.

Joshua is a passionate author, writer, editor, book designer and self-publisher to his credit are three nonfiction book he has published from www.kdp.com, US and available at www.amazon.com "Sona damsel from remote hamlet" , "Tragedy of delayed messages" and "Tragödie von verzögerten nachrichten" available on www.amazon.de (German language book). Worked as international supervisor at Johannesburg, INGO, country director for international INGO in Rwanda and Congo.

A passionate organization development professional, fund raiser also served in US. Lectured at APG university, Shimla, also at couple of colleges in Laos and presently serving as director of StStephenSchool (trust). Director Academic of Helping Life, India. Nominated as fellow of institute of Social Sciences, New Delhi and nominated as advisor, consultant and director of few other organizations, nationally and internationally. Worked with great pride and success in collaboration with United Nations, UNHCR, ICRC, UNICEF, WFP, SIDA, etc., opportunity to invite and worked with several international volunteers, orientation, briefing and engage volunteer in schedule projects task.

Joshua and Bhupinder had sleepless nights to complete this "wonder book" with idea of helping people who would like to use services ofwww.kudmai.com. Also can contact through Phone and WhatsApp:+91 7696975700. Email:bkpaul939@gmail.com. Please also visit Website for more information www.helpinglifegroup.com

Wish readers "Happy Reading" enjoy the delicious taste of Indian weddings strongly inherited and deliciously flavored with cultural diversity.Filled with fun, frolic and celebration.

Contents

1. Amazing Indian Weddings Diversity

Indian wedding is also about traditions, rituals, excitement and celebration. Nearly every aspect of a wedding has some sort of significance attached to it, whether it is traditionally applying turmeric to the bride and the groom, pledging marriage vows around the holy fire. Some of these traditions, rituals might seem trivial, but in reality, they are done for a purpose and have meaningful traditions attached to it.

Weddings have till know preserved the cultural and tradition and is great source of amusement. If you want to watch the strong impact of Indian culture, tradition and customs it is strongly visible in India wedding, rituals, ceremony and celebration. In a place like India with such diverse traditions, it is inevitable there would be too many mind-boggling rituals and traditional ceremonies when it comes to marriage. But there are mainly nine types of marriages that are largely solemnized. Indian weddings are matchless in display of culture, tradition, luxury, glory, grandeur and glamour. The other side of the story is that Indian wedding are matchless in wastage, extravagance, music, dance and display of possession of gold, money and wealth. Expensive wedding palaces are minting money from these wealthy wedding occasions. An average Indian wedding could cost between 20 lakhs (28571 USD) to 5 crores (714285USD). A person in India is estimated to spend one-fifth of the total wealth accumulated in his lifetime on his wedding. From fashion designers, event planners, florists to caterers, you need to hire an efficient team to make your special day truly incredible.

Many Indian wedding events are rooted in a time when people knew each other closely in a small, village-style community. As different communities prospered, more events were added on to the basic ceremony as visible markers of social prestige. Cropping of Several thousand wedding palaces through-out India is witness to fact that prosperity of Indians are booming and visible in India luxury class marriages.

Eighty percent of weddings happened in India are from Hindu community which are blended with strict and strong bond s of culture, tradition, nuptial customs and diversified wedding rituals. India is blessed with culturally diversified 28 Indian states and 8 Union territories. People speak different language, diversity of culture food, dress, wedding, physical appearance life style, etc. It is surprising when you travel from one state to other state there is diversity of language. Thanks to English, Hindi and Urdu language that in regional language speaking person atleast we can take the help of these three language which is mostly use in India to confabulate and make to understand each other. Sometime we have to communicate people of South and East India, within our country, in English as we cannot communicate in Hindi and regional languages.

Following are faiths practice in India Hinduism, Islam, Christianity, Sikhism , Buddhism, Jainism, Tribal Religion (incl. Sarnaism, Bon, Animism, Kirat Mundhum, Donyi-Polo) and no religion (including Atheism, Agnosticism, Secularism and Unanswered) Federal law provides official minority status to six religious groups: Muslims, Sikhs, Christians, Parsis, Jains, and Buddhists. State governments may grant minority status under state law to religious groups that are minorities in a particular region. Wedding within these religions are of its own nature with diversity in culture and tradition. Within these religion nuptial ritual are drastically marked with its own nature, style and stigma. Wedding ceremonies and celebrations are entirely different with each other. Even bride and groom are prohibited socially to get married in their own religion and are strictly barred to marry to person of other religion. But this culture is vanishing slowly due to large population of new generation, strong influence of westernization, influence of information on the life of new fast advancing generation. But still religion fanaticism is prevalent while getting married in India. It is difficult to marry in India with persons of two different religions, but some segment of India community and society who are highly educated do not bother about this while getting married.

Wedding is a powerful creator, sustainer of human and social survival for adults as well as children, about as important as literacy when it comes to promoting the health, wealth, and well-being of adults and communities. It is a symbolic gesture of our love and commitment to one another. The cause of every unhappy marriage is most likely a deep-rooted sense of unfulfillment. A feeling that there is not enough love, affection, trust, commitment, respect or other crucial components for a satisfying connection. By nature, a woman is more connected to her emotions.

The first recorded evidence of marriage ceremonies uniting one woman and one man dates from about 2350 B.C., in Mesopotamia. Over the next several hundred years, marriage evolved into a widespread institution embraced by the ancient Hebrews, Greeks, and Romans.

In India just 3 percent had a "love marriage" and another 2 percent described theirs as a "love-cum-arranged marriage", which usually indicates that the relationship was set up by the families, and then the couple agreed to get married. The word 'dowry' means the property and money that a bride brought to her husband's house at the time of her marriage. It is a custom that is prevalent in all the sections of our society in one form or the other.

2.3 million Couples wed every year in the United States. That breaks down to about 6,200 weddings per day. It comes as no surprise that the most popular wedding city in the United States is Las Vegas, with an average of 114,000 weddings per year. In 2020, Nevada had the highest marriage rate in the United States, with 21 marriages per 1,000 residents. Montana had the second highest marriage rate, at 10.4 marriages per 1,000 residents.

Couples in the United States spend the most on weddings. As of 2019, a wedding in the United States cost on average $ 29.2 thousand USD. Spain and Italy followed, with $23.4 thousand USD and $22.5 thousand USD, respectively. The study is based on interviews of couples in 14 countries worldwide. The U.S. divorce rate is amongst one of the highest in the world. There are currently over 750,000 divorces in the U.S. each year.

Guatemala has the lowest divorce rate out of all the countries globally, boasting only 0.3 divorces for every 1,000 population

Historically, the first recorded divorce in the American colonies was that of Anne Clarke and her husband Denis Clarke of the Massachusetts Bay Colony on January 5, 1643. The divorce was granted by the Quarter Court of Boston, on the grounds that Denis Clarke abandoned his wife to be with another woman.

The wedding industry generates in the United States over 60 billion dollars a year in wedding and ceremony related expenses (this figure does not include the honeymoon, which is estimated to be between 4 and 8 billion dollars a year).

A typical Indian wedding timeline stretches about three days. The Hindu wedding ceremony, which takes place on the third day, usually lasts between one-and-a-half to two hours and is then followed by the reception. The whole day clocks around 16 hours. India celebrates about 10 million weddings per year, of which about 80 percent are Hindu weddings.

There are over 10 million weddings in India every year. Estimated to be worth over $25 billion USD and growing at 30percent annually, it's one industry that hasn't seen a slowdown but always boosting.

Indian wedding ismostly split between the couple and their parents, 50/50 ratio. Sometimes however, if one side is insisting on more guests or extra fanfare, then those costs are adjusted.

Mumbai remains number one city for the most number of weddings as Delhi falls off the top three list in 2021.

India is officially considered to have one of the lowest divorce rates in the world. Indeed, if we rely on cold figures and statistical studies, it turns out that in India, only about 1 percent of all married couples end their joint family life with a dissolution of marriage.

Hindu weddings are vibrant, intricately planned, culture-rich festivities full of celebration and tradition. The marriage of Lord Shiva and Mother Parvati, Hindu God and Goddess was not an ordinary one but their ultimate destiny will be to adjust the world's greatest love stories in a moment.

Bride price, also known as bridewealth, is a token given to the bride's family by the groom's family in the form of money, gifts, valuables, etc., in order to 'seal the deal' and bond the relations between the two families through a marriage union.

Many Indian wedding events are rooted in a time when people knew each other closely in a small, village-style community. As a result, everyone had to be invited! As different communities prospered, more events were added on to the basic ceremony as visible markers of social pride and prestige. Consanguinity of marriages is prevalent in some communities in the Indian population, especially in south India. It is estimated that, at the national level prevalence of cousin marriages is 14 percent, the overall figure conceals the regional and religious differences.

Indian marriages fail due to domestic violence, gender inequality, suppression abuse and infidelity are not the only reasons why marriages break reference "Sona Damsel from

Remote Hamlet" by Joshua Irshad published by KDP, US and available of www.amazon.com. Not every fight leaves a visible scar. There are many more things that can go wrong between a married couple that only the rest of the world can't see. Sometimes, two people realize they're just not compatible. It is no surprise that India has one of the lowest divorce rate in the world. But that by no means implies that "Indian marriages are happy." It is no coincidence that married women are the highest group to commit suicide - contrary to the global trend of more men committing suicide than women.

People marry to signify a life-long commitment. to provide security for children. to make a public commitment to each other. for legal status and financial security.

On the basis of number of mates marriage may be classified into three types such as Monogamy, Polygamy and Endogamy or group marriage. According to Psychology Today, there are 7 types of marriage possibilities. Starter marriage, Companionship marriage, Parenting marriage, Safety marriage, Living alone together marriage, Living alone together marriage, Open marriage and Covenant marriage.

Dowry is illegal in India under Dowry Prohibition Act, any act to take or give dowry is punishable of imprisonment for up to 5 years and fine of Rs. 15,000 or the value of dowry given, whichever is more. Forced marriages are illegal under Article 15 of the Indian Contract Act 1872. It is a violation of human rights.

2. Wedding Ceremony Traditional Significance

Patna "turmeric ritual"

The turmeric ceremony is a ritual holy bath also known as pithi "turmeric" ceremony, which is one of the pre-wedding ceremonies in India.

Turmeric (Haldi), oil and water are applied to both the bride and groom by married women on the morning of the wedding. The mixture is believed to bless the couple before the wedding.

Sets of Bangles "Choora"

Choora (set of wedding red bangles made from elephant teeth) is ritual at bride home. On the wedding day the rituals at the girl's home begin with the Choora ceremony. The oldest maternal uncle and aunt play an important role in the performance of the ceremony. Choora is basically a set of Red bangles, gifted by girl's *mama* (mother's brother).

People touch the choora and give their heartiest wishes to the girl for her future married life. Also, they sprinkle flower petals on the bride. After that, the girl's uncle, aunt, friends and cousins tie kaliras (silver, gold or gold plated traditional ornaments) to a bangle worn by the girl.

Kaleera Ceremony

Kaleera (bride wrist wedding bangles) is tied bride-to-be to wish the newly-wed couple pleasant, happy and everlasting bond of love and affection.

Brides' sisters, her close friends and cousins tie them and wish her prosperous future life with a "silver Lining" back of every cloud she see. This remind of song by Jim Reeves, "May the good Lord bless and keep you." Kaliras remind her of her sisters, friends and relatives who she tearfully left behind after her wedding.

Jaggo "Awaken" Ceremony

In this ceremony, the family dances and sings in the beautifully decorated wedding home. Jaggo is celebrated in the last hours of the night. They decorate copper or brass vessel called khadaa(Clay pot) with diveh (clay lamps) and fill them with mustard oil and light them.

The bride or bridegroom's maternal aunt (mami) carries it on her head, and another woman will carry a long stick with bells, shaking it. The women will then go into other friends' and families' homes; after being welcomed by sweets and drinks, they dance there and move on. It is a loud ceremony, filled with joy, dancing, fireworks, and food. It is also practiced in Pakistan.

Lady Sangeet

Over the years, the sangeet (wedding ladies songs) used to last for ten days, until the wedding day. Nowadays, it has become a one day event, considering the need to conclude all wedding rites in a week.

The sangeet ceremony holds two to three days before the Mehndi (Turmeric ritual)

A groom with sehra

A groom with sehra (groom wedding head turban) ceremony

"Varna"is a ceremony that is supposed to ward off the evil eye. The groom's bhabi (sister-in-law) lines his eyes with surma (kohl). Ghodi Chadna (Wedding horse ride) is the final ceremony at the groom's place. The bride and groom are not supposed to see each other before their wedding ceremony. Therefore, a sehra solved the purpose of hiding the groom's face, whereas the bride covered her face with a ghunghat (long scraf).

The groom's sisters and cousins feed and adorn his mare. To ward off the evil eye, people use cash and perform the Varna ritual. The cash is then distributed among the poor. After this the boy climbs the horse and leaves his home for the wedding venue.

Ribbon Cutting Ceremony

When the groom cuts the ribbon, he receives the rain of flowers by the bride's women relatives. The women also perform his aarti (ritual of worship).

While ribbons tied together can symbolize a bond between a bride and groom, the cutting of a ribbon signifies a fresh start. This ceremony is full of fun and frolic from bride's sister, her cousins and close friends.

Chunni "long wedding Scarf" Escorting Ceremony

This is ceremony when the bride is brought by her bothers, cousins and close relatives to place of performing rituals and ceremonies.

Bride is given red carpet treatment in this ceremony with red decorated scarf hovering over her looks like prices strolling with her royal courtiers.

Koda Kadi "A Wedding Game"

After the wedding ceremony, it's a tradition to play games (kodakodi) to establish who will rule the roost in the marriage. In this

In this wedding game a basin is filled with milky water and inserted with ring or coin. Couple is asked to search for object thrown in basin. The one who find first will have upper hand in family affairs.

Vidaai Doli

Vidaai Doli (Farewell) is post-wedding rituals marks the departure of the bride from her parental house. As a custom, the bride throws phulian (roasted rice) or puffed rice over her head. The ritual conveys her good wishes for her parents.

A traditionally sad ritual, here the bride says goodbye to her parents, siblings and rest of her family. Her brothers/male cousins then lead her to her husband, who waits to take her to his family home to begin her new life as a married woman. Her relatives throw coins in the wake of this procession.

In keeping with tradition the mother in-law will often not come to the Doli and instead make preparations at home to greet the arrival of her son and new wife.

Milni Ritual

Milni (Introducing or meeting) Ceremony is a part of Hindu and Sikh weddings and it is held before the marriage rituals begin. Once the groom arrives from the Baraat (Wedding team) procession, he will be welcomed by the closest relatives of the bride who bless him with rose water, while offering him Shagun (gifts), a token of good luck.

In the Milni ceremony, the girl's relatives give shagun (a token of good luck) to the groom's close relatives in descending order of age. Cash and clothes are gifted.

Agni Circle

A lot of significant things happen around Agni, which is represented by having two heads, seven arms, and even seven tongues, for example the bride and groom circle Agni as they take their 7 steps wedding vows, it is important because it creates the sacred space for the ceremonial bond.

During the Saath Phere (Seven Circles), the bride and the groom, circumambulate (walk around) the sacred fire seven times as they exchange their marital vows. The fire here becomes the witness Agni Sakshi (witness) as they make promises to each other.

Sandoor Ritual

Sandoor (Vermillion) during the wedding ceremony, the groom puts sandoor on the hair parting of his bride, thereby solemnizing his sacramental union and making her his partner for life.

Sindooram is a traditional vermilion red or orange-red coloured cosmetic powder from the Indian subcontinent, usually worn by married women along the part of their hairline. In Hindu communities the sandoor is a visual marker of marital status of a woman and ceasing to wear it usually implies widowhood.

Mangalsutar ceremony

A mangala sutra (a necklace worn by a Hindu woman to signify that she is married) is a necklace that the groom ties around the bride's neck in the Indian subcontinent, in a ceremony called Mangalya Dharanam (Sanskrit for "'wearing the auspicious"').

Mangala sutra's origin dates back to the 6th Century AD as a single yellow thread was tied around the bride for protection from other men and evil spirits. Mangala sutra is a social practice widespread in India,

Chunni ceremony

The chunni (wedding scarf) ceremony is often referred to as the official engagement. The "roka" is an informal engagement when the couple are blessed and recognized by both families as to-be-weds. The chunni cements this and makes them official fiancés.

The bride's family will do the kurmai ceremony for the groom. The groom's family will do the chunni ceremony for the bride. The kurmai can be said as the principal ceremony of the engagement in the Punjabi wedding. This ritual can be arranged at the groom's place or the religious places.

Sgan ceremony

Sagan(wedding gifts of good luck) is an event that marks the auspicious beginning of the couples' lives.

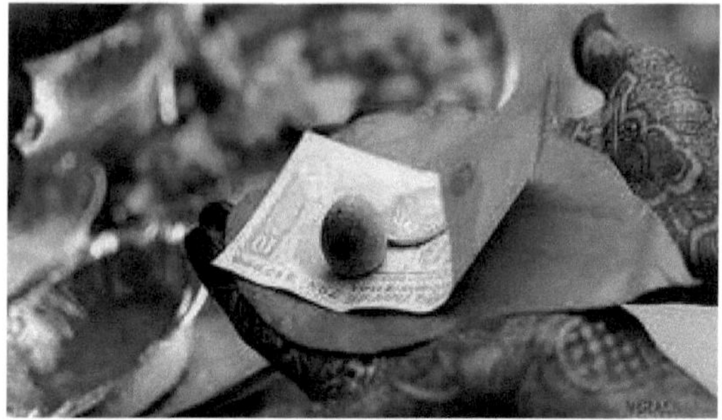

The girl's relatives give shagun (a token of good luck) to the groom's close relatives in descending order of age. Cash and clothes are gifted.

Jaimala ritual

The jaimala is a token of acceptance. When the bride and the groom exchange the garland, it symbolizes the acceptance of would-be man by the would-be wife as her partner for life.

This tradition has been in practice since the Ramayana and the Mahabharata days.

Vadai Ritual

This ritual of throwing rice and coins symbolizes that she is repaying back her parents for keeping her in the house. This ceremony is rented with tears and sadness on the side of bride and her family.

Vadai or Bidaai is the Hindu customs in which after marriage, the bride walks out with the Groom from her parent's home into a new world to lay the foundation for an entire new life with new family and a different environment.

Welcome Couple

However, at the welcome reception of bride-in-law home, most bride and groom couples are given a glorious welcome to make her grand entrance into the new home which belong to her husband.

There are few ceremonies preformed when bride enter and start her new life. This is the time when the bride is given a warm welcome from her in-laws. The entry is almost identical just like in other cultures- as the bride is to enter the house with her right foot first which is thought to be propitious. After entering, the bride is welcomed by her mother-in-law with an Aarti (traditional religious worship).

3. Castles'land, Wedding Of Rajasthan

Rajasthan is best described as land of Castles, Forts, Kings, Queens, Prince, Princes and Kingdoms, architectural wonders, cultural extravaganza, fabulous history and warm hospitality.

It is Incredible land of colorful mélange of massive forts, diverse culture, stunning palaces and delectable cuisines. It is well known for great hospitality and invites guests with melodious, beautiful song with theme "please come to my land." Amalgamation of splendid folk dance and music, typically dressed women dances, golden sand desert, camels, colorful and large men turbans make it an awesome place. A visit to Rajasthan is the complete bouquet for the vivid experience and perfect global unique place for royal style wedding offered by www.kudmai.com.

Capital "Pink" city, Jaipur flooded with majestic forts, palaces, lakes and monuments, architectural glories and has many other attractions thrillinghamlets visitations of the royal state is alternate way to taste the blissful beauty of the place.This majestic state displaysfragrance of cultural opulence everywhere. Cities in urban locality of the state are still closely associated with the old culture and tradition preserving the legacy of the past. Fairs,festivals that reflect the old traditionsand rituals are amazingly unbelievable to eyes.

The praiseworthy history of Rajasthan is about 5000 years old. The downfall of well- established Gupta Empire marks the inception of Rajputana, popping up a cluster of several Princely States of Rajasthan. The situation improved at the time of independence when Rajputana majorly comprised of 18 princely states joined hands with each other. The year 1950 mark the merger of all 18 princely provinces into one united Sates of Rajasthan and Maharaja of Jaipur Sawai Man Singh II was elected as the Rajpramukh.

Bestowed with varying environmental and topographic features, the major parts of the state are dominated by parched and dry region. The extensive topography includes rolling sand dunes, rocky terrain, land filled with thorny scrubs, wetlands, plateaus and wooded regions. The state is home to the Great Indian Thar Desert.

Another feather in the hat of enchanting glorious Rajasthan is its authentic civilization and rich culture that vibrantly speak Its cultural heritage is also rich and perhaps carefully nurtured over centuries Rajasthani arts and crafts are beyond comparison and famous across the globe. Its traditional jewellery, ornaments, precious stones and artistically design gold ornament speak volume about Rajasthan richness in jewellery craft.

Along with rich heritage, culture, magnificent forts and palaces; one of the major attractions of Rajasthan is delicious and finger licking cuisine. The state makes its traveller happy from every corner whether by entertaining or by serving delectable food. Traditional cuisines of Rajasthan are very much popular among visitors. Delicious traditional culinary dishes are worth to taste and royal guest treatment.

Wedding at Umaid Bhawan PalaceRajasthan

Desert wedding dance entertainment

Umaid Bhawan Palace Rajasthan

Royal wedding atUmaid Bhawan Palace

Rajasthan royal wedding in Castle

Rajasthan traditional dance & celebration

Rajasthani wedding glamour of traditional dress and jewellery

Bride of royal land of Rajasthan

Royal weedding in the castle

Charmand grace of Rajasthan bride

Rajasthan Bride loaded with jewellery ornaments

Rajasthan Couple after wedding

Rajasthan Bride with wedding jewellery

Royal Wedding of Rajasthan

Bride dressed and decked for her Wedding

Traditional wedding ornament Rajasthan

Rajasthan traditional wedding feast

Red Lamb meat on wedding feast

Rajasthan traditional Wedding dance

Rituals, Ceremonies and Cultural Heritage of Rajasthan's Weddings

In this chapter exploredRajasthani wedding traditions across state and microscopically looking into the royal and heritage wedding style.

Royalty, rich cultural heritage and a magnificent lifestyle are the reflection of the Rajasthan. Weddings from the desert state are truly with the opulent decorations, vibrant colors, traditional and folk dance form and music.

Weddings is practiced in differently in Rajasthani communities who have different traditions and customs. Each more colorful and magnificent than the other. As much as the base traditions remain the same, their way of expressing them can be quite different. You can see classic examples of this in Rajasthani wedding traditions from the Rajput community.

Rajput Wedding Traditions are conventionally, the warrior class is known for rich and royal Rajasthani weddings. You can see the display of velour in modern-day weddings, whether it's in the groom carrying a sword or riding on a horse or elephant at the head of his Baraat (Groom wedding team) . Each Rajput family has its own set of values that frame their wedding rituals making it a grand royal affair.

Here are some Rajasthani wedding traditions that are specific to this community.

The Tilak (Religion mark) ceremony in the Rajasthani wedding is an equivalent of the traditional Roka (Fixed) ceremony, where the impending marriage is officially announced. A male ceremony, the men from the bride-to-be's home bear gifts for the groom and his family (a sword, clothes, jewellery, sweets). The bride's brother anoints the groom with a Tilak. This is nowadays, followed by an exchange of rings at a ring ceremony or Sagaai (Engagement).

Ganpati (Hindu God of wisdom) Sthapana (Establishment) ritual where no Shubh (lucky) event is organized amid Hindu traditions without invoking the Gods. And here, this is done by inviting Lord Ganesh (Hindi God) to come home and bless the wedding. In this ceremony, an idol of Lord Ganesha is welcomed into the home for prayers.

Pithi Dastoor(Turmeric ritual) involves a variant of the well-loved Haldi (Henna) ceremony in Rajasthani wedding where the bride and the groom are the playful victims. Relatives apply Haldi paste on the bride and groom. This paste has turmeric and sandalwood in it which bring glowing and radiant skin before the big day. Yellow is the colour of the event and yellow is also related to holiness in some Indian religions.

Rajputi 'Mehfil'(Gathering) is the music and dance night, or the Sangeet(Wedding songs)ceremony. Traditionally, this is the night when the bride and the groom side all come together to enjoy the traditional form of dance. These days, we see it becoming into a performance night when relatives and friends prepare and perform their own bits for all to enjoy.

Mahira Dastoor(skilled ceremony) is a fun and frolic ceremony, the 'Mama' (Maternal Uncle) brings gifts for the bride/groom and their families. Traditionally it symbolizes that he is also sharing the expense of the wedding.

Palla (bride outer garment), Janev (Sacred Hindu thread) ceremony is of unique nature. The Palla ceremony is done in the early hours of the wedding day. Groom's side comes to visit the bride with gifts of clothing and jewellery. Janev ceremony also takes place at the groom's place where he is dressed is saffron and performs a ceremony before putting an orange thread around his neck. This embarks their acceptance for the new marital life.

Nikasi (Groom wedding turban ritual) is the Sehra(Wedding turban) ceremony where the groom's sisters tie a golden thread Sehra around the groom's head and then apply a black Kajal (kohl) to ward off any evil. This is right before the Barat ceremony.

Varmala (wedding garland) and Pheras (sacred wedding rounds) is contrary to the general practice of 7 Pheras at the mandap (platform for wedding), a Rajasthani wedding only has 4 Pheras at the mandap when they circle around the holy fire and the remaining three are taken later at the entrance of the bride's new house where she is going to spend rest of her life.

Satapadi (7 sacred steps) ritual in which bride and groom take seven steps together. Each of these steps represents a promise that they make to each other showing the commitment to each other.

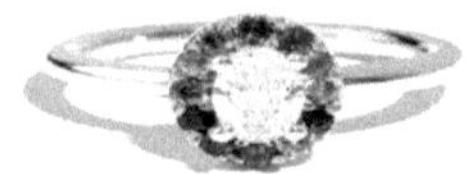

4. Himachal

Himalayas Wedding

Himachal Pradesh is a northern Indian state in the Himalayas. It's home to scenic mountain towns, orchards and resorts. Host to the Dalai Lama, Himachal Pradesh has a strong Tibetan presence. This is reflected in its Buddhist temples and monasteries, as well as its vibrant Tibetan New Year celebrations at place. The region is also well known for paragliding, its trekking, climbing and skiing areas. Popularly renowned for its Himalayan landscapes, lush green meadows and popular hillstations. Many outdoor activities such as rock climbing, mountain biking, paragliding, ice-skating, trekking, rafting, trout fishing, camping and heli-skiing are popular attractions in Himachal Pradesh.

The state is mainly mountainous, but the southern part is made of fertile plains. Rivers and glaciers irrigate the state, and there is extensive terrace farming of rice and fruits in Himachal. The major rivers are Chenab, Ravi, Sutlej, Beas and Yamuna. There is extensive forest cover in this state and Alpine, as well as evergreen forests spread out extensively.

Himachal is inhabited by semi-nomadic tribes like the Gaddis, Gujjars, Kinnars, Lahaulis and Pangwals (all tribal nomads). People of Himachal, commonly known as

Himachalis, are very warm and friendly and the love to welcome visitors.

Most people living in the trans-Himalayan areas such as Lahaul and Spiti, Kinnaur and Kullu follow Buddhism. Himachalis celebrate fairs and festivals throughout the year with dance and music.

The majestic Himalayas stand tall in the state of Himachal which is located in the Dhauladhar range, one of the mid-Himalayan ranges. Many festivals celebrate the mountain and river deities and have become part of the Himachali culture. Manali is among one of the most popular travellers destinations, not only in the state of Himachal Pradesh but in India.

Being located in the foothills of the Himalayas, the evergreen forests are well watered and are rich in flora and fauna. The forests of Himachal are also home to some treasured medicinal plants that are now being used in pharmaceuticals.

There are around 20 state-level fairs that take place in Himachal that are recognized by the government. Naina Devi Fair, Lavi Fair, Chrewal, Renuka Fair, Chintpurni Fair and the Nalwari Fair are some of the fairs held in Himachal.

Wedding celebrations, rituals and ceremonies of Himachal are full of fun, frolic and lively spirit. Where love for music,dance, traditional ceremonies and rituals dominate wedding celebrations.

Culture, traditions and customs are strongly visible in weddings which happen in mountain state of Himachal. Wedding in remotest region of Himachal are worth watching. Bride and bridegroom during wedding are colorfully dressed up. Himachal is also know place of God and Goddess.

Himachal Bride Traditionally dressed

Hilarious moments after wedding rituals

The Tribal wedding and tribal bride

Himachal tribal smiling bride

Himachal bride ready for wedding occasion

Traditional wedding feast

Traditional wedding jewellery

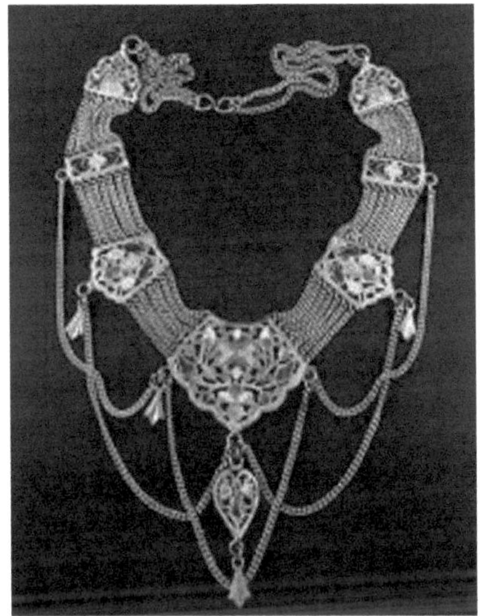

Wedding traditional remote region dance

Musical wedding traditional instruments

Rituals, Ceremonies and Cultural Heritage of Himachal's Weddings

A Himachali bride will always tell you about the many traditions and rituals before, during and after a wedding. Himachali wedding traditions are very simple yet extremely meaningful. There's something about a Himachali wedding and the experience a Himachali bride goes through that has always made it a little more fascinating. The weddings in the woods have always been a tale to tell and a "Once upon a time" fairytale that is a dream come true to be a part of even as a spectator or a guest if not the bride herself.

Dogra Nath, the traditional nose ring that all Himachali brides wear with pride. It is an elaborate nose ring that is the mark of a married woman in Himachal. No special occasion, festival or celebrations are complete without adorning this beautiful piece of jewellery.

One of the most important rituals and the ceremony is the 'Mama (maternal uncle) Swagat (welcome)'. Mama, or mother's brother, plays an important role in a Himachali bride's wedding. The maternal uncles and aunts shower the Himachali bride with gifts, blessing and officially declare the start of the wedding ceremonies. The Mama of the Himachali bride also gifts her a traditional Chunri (long wedding scraf), another mark of a married woman.

This is followed by the Halad or Haldi (turmeric) ceremony. Haldi, or turmeric, is a natural herb that is powdered and mixed with sandalwood powder and milk to form a paste. This paste is then applied on the bride's face, arms and legs. Yes, it's the most ancient form of wedding beauty treatments. The Haldi ceremony is crazy and also very emotional one for bride. All Mamas and Mamis (maternal aunty), cousins and friends painted bride with yellow Haldi. It is was such a beautiful day with all loved ones around bride, blessing and showering bride with all their love. This follow with dance for hours, blended eating Himachali food which make bride to feel as the queen in the castle.

On the wedding day, all the men of the bride's family wear a Sehra (Groom wedding turban). The wedding party then gets ready for the Saptapadi(7 sacred wedding steps), the welcoming ceremony for the groom's family. Gifts and sweets are given to the groom's side to welcome them.

During the wedding ritual, red cloth is tied to the groom's and the bride's dress. This knot signifies the union of the couple. This is followed by the 7 Pheras (sacred rounds), each a promise that the couple makes to one another.

And then the most difficult, emotional yet beautiful ceremony, the Kanyadaan (bride handover) and Vidai (bid farewell). Kanyadaan and Vidai are emotional and traditional wedding rituals where the bride's parents officially give the bride to the groom and bid her farewell for her new home and life. A Himachali bride goes through a whirlwind of emotions during her wedding.

5. Wedding in Paradise Kashmir

Srinagar is a globally renowned hill destination in India famed for its lakes, waterways, centuries old Mughal gardens, and a town that is blended with rich heritage and where, culture, traditional, crafts lavish traditional culinary tremendously flourish. Once a favorite destination, Srinagar went through 2 decades of political unrest, which now is completely diminished. Beautiful valley, nature and local People welcoming and generously extend warmth, courtesies to the visitors. Co-author Joshua Irshad is born, educated in Jammu and Kashmir, married in Srinagar. During his wedding there was great traditional feast of Wazwaan from girl side as a courtesy to wedding visitors.

Everlasting romance with Kashmir secretly begin with salubrious weather, glorious sunshine and delightful rounds of ride on the deep green lake water on the Dal Lake, Nagin Lake, numerous rounds of savoring 'Kehwa', Kashmiri saffron tea made in traditional Swanwar, sitting on the patio of the Houseboat on the Dal Lake.

The graceful solace of refreshing misty morning rejuvenate the mind and spirit. All this give impression like "Alice in Wonderland", the moment we land in "Paradise", a land of eternal bliss.

Dal lake is not only home sweet home to beautiful local houseboats, shikaras (lake passenger boats), but also it is temporary home to visitors, families, who wish to spend time in Paradise.

Innovative flourishing floating vegetable farms on the Dal lake water produces local organic vegetables full of freshness and unique taste. Every morning a temporary floating vegetable market springs up around the sunrise, witnesses quick deals and off-loading of sold vegetables onto the empty boats of buyers and make way towards the boulevard for onward transporting to the downtown Srinagar. Hilarious floating organic vegetable farmers after hectic business trip heading back home in boats after selling off their fresh stock.

Flowers sellers on Dal Lake are a so charming to eyes, visible rowing their flower filled boat moving from one houseboat to another in search of a customers for their beautiful fragmented flowers. These beautiful flowers tempt one in buying a bunch of them to place in flower vase in houseboat's drawing room and bed rooms.

Spending enchanting nights inglorious Houseboats on the Dal Lake or Nagin Lake. Houseboat is luxurious rich experience self- contained well equipped furnished for a comfortable stay available on board.

A typical floating houseboat has two to three bedrooms with an en suite bathroom, a spacious Living room, a dining room, pantry and a front lounge. Some houseboats have adjoining small garden or a on the water deck, where one can sun bathe or just relax. The houseboats are richly furnished with carpets, Kashmiri handicrafts and ornate woodwork designs on the ceiling and walls of any houseboat.

Lovely houseboats are classified into category depending on the amenities available on board. These houseboats are closer to Mughals emperor Nishat, Shalimar Gardens, Char (four) Chinar (Maple), Dal Market, Floating vegetable market and lotus farms.

A dictum from Mughal Emperor in appreciation of beauty of Kashmir

Emperor Jahangir had once said about Kashmir, "Agar firdaus bar roo-e zameen ast, Hameen ast-o, hameen ast-o, hameen ast! (If there is a paradise on earth; it is this, it is this, it is this)."

Boat flowers vendor in Dal Lakes, Srinagar selling flowers

Houseboats for Weddings occasion

Bride from Kashmir Valley dressed for wedding

Kashmiri bride in traditional wedding gold jewellery and dress

Bride in traditional Kashmiri ornaments and head gears

A Pretty Kashmiri Bride in Wedding Kashmiri Jewellery

Wazwaan traditional weeding food during Kashmiri Weddings

Wazwaan wedding feast, Kashmiri Weddings cooked in special Kashmiri Utensils

Christian Wedding in Srinagar, Kashmir, All Saint Church, pretty Neena

Kashmiri bride supporting traditional gold jewellery on the her wedding occasion

Kashmiri Wedding party in Srinagar in a wedding Resort

Kashmiri traditional Wedding Jewellery

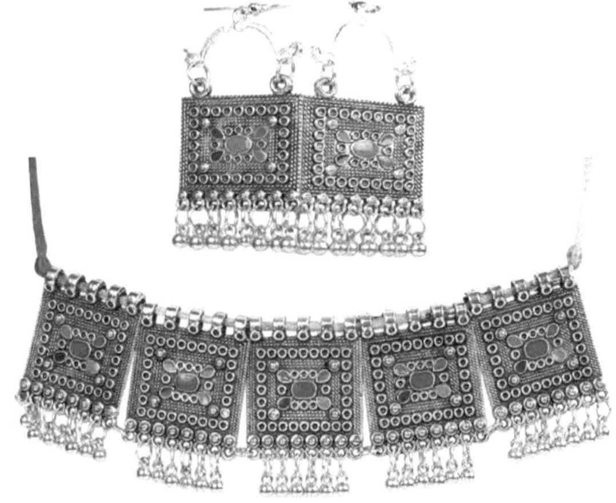

Five Stars houseboat in Dal Lake, Srinagar, Kashmir worth for weddings ceremonies

Rituals, Ceremonies and Cultural Heritage of Kashmir's Weddings

The culture, tradition and custom of Kashmir was influenced by the Persian as well as Central Asian Kashmiri culture is strongly influenced by Hinduism, Buddhism and later by Islam. Kashmir's nuptial rituals that blend with amazing ceremonies are so charming.

Weddings in "Paradise" Kashmir are of unique nature, rituals, ceremonies and celebrations garnished with joyful festivities, fun and frolic. Obviously blend with rich wedding traditions. Kashmiri weddings are truly a great occasion of celebration, display of rich culture, traditions and customs.

Kashmir is also known as "Little Switzerland", also called as "Paradise", and sometime "Kashmir as heaven on earth" and the wedding in Kashmir are more like a match fixed in heaven.

The wedding ceremonies initially begin withManzimyor (Matchmaker) is a Kashmiri word. Family hires a Manzimyor to find suitable profiles of both boys and girls to be future couple. The matchmaker shares the best suitable profiles, according to need, of the eligible brides and grooms with the family in a process called "Parche Traavum."

Thap traavun (Both party agreed) Final official yes for the nuptial knot. After matching the horoscopes and meeting the respective sides, the family then officially announces the wedding. The groom's family adorns the bride with a lot of gold jewellery and "Poend"(Gold coin).

Nishayn (Engagement) is followed after "Thap Traavun" ceremony, both the family organize a grand ceremony called Nishayn or engagement, organized by the bride's family. Close family members and friends are invited for this ritual. The ceremony is followed by a delicious exotic lavish feast called "Wazwaan".

Then comes Saatnaam (7th days later bring bride home) after the Nishayn rituals the family conclude, officially announces the wedding dates to the family and friends. Saatnaam, too is a grand celebration with traditional folk dance, songs, music and lavish Kashmiri meals.

Malmaenz(turmeric) Malmaenz, also known as maun or haldi. The families start off the main wedding ceremonies with malmaenz. Elder women in the families oil bride's hair and applies turmeric to her.

Maenzraat (heena) is Kashmiri tradition, the night before the wedding isMaenzraat, where the women in family apply mehendi or henna on the bride's hands, exposed arms and feet.

Ab Shehrun (Special bridal bath and Namaz) in the morning of the wedding day, the bride takes a bath to cleanse herself for the new beginnings. She is mostly accompanied by her mother or sisters. After the bath, the bride wears their traditional outfit called Pehran (long gown) and offers two rakath(Wedding attire).

Nikah Khwaani (Muslim agreement) the Nikah in Kashmiri tradition is the most modest one. The priest recites holy verses of Quran and prays for the happiness of the bride and groom.

Yiniwol(The Feast) Post the wedding, the families, friends, neighbors gather together for lunch and bless the couple.

"Mehraaz Saal",in the evening, the groom and the baratis (groom wedding team) are given a royal treatment where they are served food in beautiful copper plates. And the groom is given an extravagant seat made of silk carpets.

Ruksati (bride departure), after the dinner, the bride finally bids goodbye to her family and embarks on a new journey of life with her husband. This ceremony is very touching where a bride spend best slice of her life at parents' home, but finally shift to new home and environments. Shedding of tears, sobbing and sadness rent the ritual of Ruksati.

"Muhar Tullun"(Bride scarf lifting ritual) the groom's mother welcomes the bride to her new house and family and lifts the veil from her face. Family members and relatives give precious gifts to the bride and women sing traditional wedding songs.

Walima(Grand reception), followed by a feast held by the groom's family where they invite their friends, family members and their community.

"Khabri Gasun",after a few days of the wedding, the bride's relatives except her parents visit the groom's house to bless them and give gifts to them, mostly cash.

"Phiri Saal", after the wedding, the bride's family invites both the bride and the groom for dinner, treat them with the utmost love and honour.

Satim Doh (7th day of post wedding), for ensuing seven days after the wedding, the bride wears seven different colours for seven days and does no household chores. After the seventh day, the bride's parents are invited to the groom's place for dinner and the day is called "Satim Doh". After which the bride goes to her parent's house for a few days.

Phirraa Khaber (Bride's relatives after2 days visit her with gifts, to know about her welfare), after the bride returns from to her in-law's house, their relatives come to visit them to make sure she is doing well.

The formal commitment ceremony in true Kashmiri tradition, Kasamdry(Vow) is held at a temple. The families meet and exchange flowers and offer puja to acknowledge the match, after which they enjoy a traditional Lagan the Kashmiri wedding ceremony is known as lagan. It follows all the normal Vedic rituals. The priest performs a Mandap (holy fire)puja followed by the Dwar puja before ushering in the groom. The bride is carried to the wedding mandap by her maternal uncle.

Vegetarian meal prepared by the bride's family.Kashmiri weddings are traditionally a grand affair that last around four to five days.This involves a couple of scrumptious 12-course feasts (Kashmiri wazwaan) and a large gathering of friends and relatives who breathe life into the party.

These days, Kashmiri brides also choose to opt for a bridal saree (long coloured bride wrapper) or lehenga (lady jumper) instead of the complete Pheran (Kasmiri traditional gown). The bride also wears an elaborate headgear known as Kasaba. Heavy pins and trinkets are worn to hold the headgear in right place. To complete the look an embroidered dupatta(Lady scarf) over the head is worn by the bride. Taranga (Kashmiri taringi is the typical headscarf) worn by Kashmiri Pandit women until the late 1960s. Now its only place is as a ritual and by tradition to be worn in a classical way on the bride's head as a bridal gear on her wedding day.

The bride-to-be was laden in new jewellery by her family along with a ritual where her hair was braided into tiny braids. The Masmuchrun ritual is significant in Kashmiri weddings, where the elder women of the family oil the bride's hair and tie them in tiny braids. Jiggni (forehead bride ornament in different shape) and Tikka (Gold round ornament hang on forehead) are the types of Kashmiri head jewellery. These are worn on the forehead, are generally triangular, semi-circular, and circular in shape. These are made of gold and silver and are fringed with hanging pearls and gold leaves.

Wazwaan, the Kashmiri cuisine, is a unique and inseparable component of Kashmiri culture. It comprises from seven to 36 dishes of mutton or beef, chicken, fruits, and vegetables. The important ethnic meat products of wazwaan include kabab, tabak maaz, aab gosh, rogan josh, nate-yakhni, rista, and goshtaba.

Dejhoor(Ornament a sign of wedding)is an ornament worn by Kashmiri Hindu brides, from the day before they are wed in holy matrimony. The jewelry is hung off of the ear and later is replaced with a gold chain known as an ath at her to-be husband's home. The athur (Ornament), which is a small gold ornament, is added attached to the dejhoor.

During Devgon (fire puja) ceremony. In this Kashmiri ritual, water, rice, milk, and curd are poured over the bride's head, while young girls hold a veil over the bride's head. And the maternal uncle gifts the bride a new set of clothes,which was followed by the Masmuchrun ceremony.

Thus in Kashmir a middle class wedding costs INR 7-10 lakh(9729 USD to 14285 USD), the upper class ones INR 10-20 lakh (14285 USD to 28571 USD) and poor also INR 2-3 lakhs (2857 USD to 4285 USD)Additionally many book marriage halls, hotels, professional singers etc. which can also cost 1-2 lakh(1428 USD to 4285 USD).

6. Traditional

Kerala Nuptials

Kerala, a Southern state on India's tropical Malabar Coast, has nearly 600kmof Arabian Sea shoreline. It's known for its palm-lined beaches and backwaters, a network of canals. Inland are the Western Ghats, mountains whose slopes support tea, coffee and spice plantations as well as wildlife. Kerala is home to elephants, langur monkeys and tigers. Ranked ninth among the best tourism websites in the world.According to the world rankings of tourism related websites extracted from www.alexa.com, Kerala Tourism ranks ninth among the best tourism websites in the world, closely followed by Mauritius Tourism and Cyprus Tourism.

Named as one of the ten paradises of the world by National Geographic Traveler, Kerala is famous especially for its ecotourism and beautiful backwaters. Its unique culture and traditions, coupled with its varied demography, have made Kerala one of the most popular place in the world.

Classical art forms, colorful festivals, exotic cuisine are some of the cultural marvels that await travellers. Ayurveda, the ancient Indian system of medicine and Panchakarma, the rejuvenation therapy in Ayurveda have also helped Kerala to gain a pan-global reputation as a worth-visit destination.

Season never ends in Kerala, thanks to the year-long moderate climate and numerous festivals and events.

A traditionally made hotel boat of Kerala

Local Boats and Coconuts Trees

Kerala cuisine is a culinary style originated in the Kerala, a state on the southwestern Malabar Coast of India. Kerala cuisine offers a multitude of both vegetarian and non-vegetarian dishes prepared using fish, poultry and red meat with rice as a typical accompaniment. Chillies, curry leaves, coconut, mustard seeds, turmeric, tamarind, asafoetida and other spices are also used in the preparation.

Kerala is known as the "Land of Spices" because it traded spices with Europe as well as with many ancient civilizations with the oldest historical records.

Because of its rich trading heritage, over time, various indigenous Kerala dishes have been blended with foreign dishes to adapt them to local tastes. Coconuts grow in abundance in Kerala, so grated coconut and coconut milk are commonly used for thickening and flavoring. Having been a major production area of spices for thousands of years, the region makes frequent use of black pepper, cardamom, clove, ginger, and cinnamon. Kerala also has a variety of breakfast dishes like idlis (Savory rice cake)served with local vegetables made sauces and dosa(flatten Indian bread from rice batter filled with mixed).

Amazing traditional Kerala style wedding are very entertaining with festive celebrations, magnificent blend of customized traditional dresses, food, music, dances and cultural wedding ceremonies.

In the Nair ceremony, the 'Kanyadaan' is followed by 'Pudamuri,' where the groom gifts his bride a saree and blouse on a platter, signifying that he will provide for her for the rest of her life. The couple exchange garlands and are blessed with gifts as the bride's father officially hands her over to the groom. The mainstay of a Kerala wedding for a Nair couple is loosely termed the Kanyadaan. It begins with a ceremonial welcome for the groom and his family, followed by the blushing bride's beatific entry.

A wedding in Kerala can cost you anywhere from INR 2.5 Lakhs to 20 Lakhs depending on your taste. Wealthy families spend more with pomp and show. If you want to know wealth of a person it is displayed during wedding.

Kerala dress code for the bride consists of the famous Kasavu saree which is an all plain-white saree with golden border. Kasavu saree is considered as the most auspicious form of Kerala dress that woman also wear for special occasions apart from adorning it on every Hindu new year. The brides wear a traditional saree as well as a plethora of gold jewellery.

The traditional jewellery of Kerala includes the very beautiful maanga maala (Mango Necklace), kaasu mala (Coin Chain or Necklace), Lakshmi kadas (Wealth Necklace), and necklaces, and a wide variety of engraved ornaments. They carry ethnic and spiritual meanings, especially during weddings.

The pieces of jewelries worn by the bride signifies that she is to become a part of her husband's extended family. They are a part of the purification ritual as she becomes a part of the extended family of her bridegroom.

Kerala people are so obsessed with gold and gold jewellery because they believe that Goddess laxmi (Goddess of wealth) brings more prosperity and shower her blessing to their lives if they buy gold

Most of Indian brides traditionally wear red and white bangles. White bangles are made of conch shells while the red bangles are made of red corals. It is believed that the bride has to be careful not to break these bangles during the first year of marriage and if it does, it is considered as a bad omen. Traditionally there are 21 bangles, although more recently the bride often wears 7, 9 or 11 bangles. The bangles range in size according to the circumference of the top of the forearm and the wrist end so that the set fits neatly.

Bestowed with a pleasant and equable climate throughout the year, Kerala is a tropical land where one can relax and be at ease. The generally pleasant climate prevalent here is what our guests end up loving.

The wild lands are covered with dense forests, while other regions lie under tea and coffee plantations or other forms of cultivation. Most of the state is engulfed in rich greenery which ensures a very calming experience at all times.

It has Midlands of undulating hills and valleys into an unbroken 580 km long coastline with Indian Ocean. Therefore Kerala has got hills and beaches both blend into beautiful toenjoy.

Keralabride in traditional handmade cotton saree teamed with gold emboridrees

Couple in traditional wedding costumes

Alluring aroma of Jasmine decorates in bride hairs

Twenty-five verities Kerala traditional wedding food served on concluding day

Kerala bride wears 320 grams of gold, the highest among brides in the country

Traditional Wedding Jewellery

Captivating Sunset of Kerala

Rituals, Ceremonies and Cultural Heritage of Orissa's Weddings

Most of the South Indian Hindu weddings are common in celebrative culture, traditions and rituals, but there are some ceremonies which are distinctive to Malayali wedding. Malyali (Kerala) wedding is more delightful and cultural bond than other states of South India. Even if the wedding is held by rich affluent parents in seven stars properties, where swaying palm trees, expensive beaches, tranquil backwaters, lush green farm and myriad culture. Even than the glory and grace of traditional wedding is not missing inspite of introduction of modern facilities at these expensive places.

Pre- Nuptial blessing help ceremony help a day before the wedding, the pre-nuptial ceremony involves the bride and bride and bridegroom receiving blessings from their loved ones at functions hosted in their respective homes It is often followed by a feast.

While most wedding ceremonies in other regional cultures of India take place in the evening of night, couple from Kerala typically tie the knot early in the morning as that particular time is considered to be the most culturally auspicious according to practiced belief.Kerala weddings, traditions, customs, rituals style and other amazing ceremonies related to Hindu Malayai weddings. This book explore the nuances and rituals of traditional Hindu Malayali wedding. Kerala weddings are quite different in it celebrative nature from other part of India, be it in term of bridal make up. Bridal look, décor, cultural coloured ceremonies at the time of nuptials. Even these traditional weddings have their own taste of distinct array of eye brows raising memorable rituals.During wedding series of cheerful pleasant ceremonies the first ceremony after the fixing of the wedding is "Nichayan" ceremony marks the official engagement where the two families exchange the matched horoscope and also gifts. After this follow the "Mothiram Maattal" which is known as ring ceremony.

Mehndi (Henna) The ceremony of Mehndi performed at the wedding commences with the bride's aunts applying the first few touches of Henna to her hands before professional Mehndi (henna) artists take over their intricate design on front and back side of hands , also half arms are covered drawing of Henna with beautiful designs.

While most norms of Malayali weddings that jewelry display is quite visible and ride is decorated with it. From forehead jewellery ornament to waist belts, bangles, bracelets, necklaces, earning rings as a result bride is all about opulence when it comes to her wedding jewellery. Temple jewellery swap out diamonds along with meenakari (Enameling) and pearl ornaments for some gold bling when hosting a Malayali wedding. Ornaments carved into traditional intricate designs with sure touch of traditions these gold splendid creation blend a regal touch to any outfit. Men can look the part of y wearing traditional Mundus (White and gold embroidered dhotis). Pair it with short and long Kurta (Shirt) in white or other related traditional colour.

"Madhuparkam" ceremony is in which the groom's feet are washed by the bride's father and other relatives when groom arrives for the wedding ceremony. He then presents the bride's father with a white Kasavu saree (Gold thread long bride wrapper) that she has to wear during the wedding.

The quintessential white and gold sarees introduced to weddings, creation includes handwoven white and cream cotton saress that are embroidered with pure gold zari threadwork. Bridesmaids and guest give a sarees known as Kasavu (Gold Thread) saree their hand made team it up with a colorful blouse and gold bling. In Nair caste in Kerala the ceremonies of "Kanyadaan " is followed by " Pudamuri" where the groom gifts his bride a saree and blouse on a platter, signifying that he will provide her for the rest of her life. The couple exchange floral garlands and are blessed with gifts as the bride's father official hands her over to the groom.

Bridegroom during wedding weave the delicate beauty and alluring aroma of native white jasmine bunch of flowers tugged into their coconuts oiled glistening long jet black hairs with Gajras (Floral garland of Jasmine) that have been cultural , traditional part of Indian bridal looks during auspicious occasion of brides' pride. Bride look charming and perfect with large low and high beautiful buns, braids and open wavy tresses.

Sadhya (Twilight) Lunch, the traditional meal of twenty five delicious food items served on plantain leaves, the pure vegetarian lunch concluded the wedding festivities and extended celebration. The delicious lavish pure vegetarian meal that marks the culmination of the wedding is the greatest highlight of Kerala wedding festivities. Traditionally served on tree leaf.This verities of meal contains of par boiled rice, a wide array of vegetables and curries, savories such as pappadam (Indian flatbread) and khichdi (rice and lentils), pickles, fruit, buttermilk and also desert.

Sparsham (The Touch) is concluded wedding ritual, the groom and the bride sit on the ground facing each other with their foreheads touching. The bride pours rice into the holy fire as the priest chants religious wedding verses from Hindu religious book. After this the groom puts the bride's foot on the grinding stone that symbolizes her leaving her family for a new home.

Kanyadaanam (daughter handover) is much like other Indian cultures, the Malayali wedding includes a giving away ceremony involving the bride. This ceremony called Kanyadaanam, it is performed around a Veli (holy fire). The couple have to take three rounds of fire after which the bride's father hands the groom a "Taali" (Metal Plate) known as "Mangalsutra" (Cultural Necklace) to tie around the bride's neck in a ritual known as "Taalikettu" (Wedding String Ceremony).

Kudivep and Griha Pravesh is ritual unlike many other culture, the Malayali weddings do not include a "bidaai" (Bridal Farewell). Instead, the ritual of "Griha Pravesh" focuses on the happy chapter of the bride arriving at her new home. The custom of grooms' mother welcoming the newly-wed couple with "Diyas" (earthen lamps) is called "Kudevep" after which the bride enters the home with her right foot while carrying a lamp which is symbolic of her bringing new light into the house.

7. Ladakh Buddhist

Wedding Ceremony

Ladakh, sometimes referred to as Little Tibet, is popular with travellers because it is home to one of the purest remaining examples of Tibetan Buddhist culture. Visitors come to see a preindustrial culture, tour the Buddhist monasteries, and take in the dramatic mountain vistas.

Their culture is rich and colorful, centering around the beliefs and practices of Tibetan Mahayana Buddhism, the predominant religion. Ladakh and the tiny kingdom of Bhutan , are perhaps the purest remaining examples of traditional Tibetan societies.

About life of people in Ladakh, they traditionally lead a nomadic rustic life and are sincere and honest. Ninety percent of them depend on agriculture based on the Indus River for their livelihood. Their main agricultural products are barley, wheat, buckwheat, peas, rapeseed and beans.

The Ladakh festival is a blend of various cultures of Central Asian, Tibetan and Northern India, which are all found in Ladakh.

Ladakhi people believe in the power of stones. These are prized not only for their beauty but also for their significance. The stones which dominate the necklaces, bracelets, earrings and waist belts are turquoise and corals. Pearls, lapis lazuli, amber and quartz crystals are also used but these have less importance.The attires of Ladakh, people wear a thick woolen robe called Goncha (the traditional gown) with accessories such as Tipi (hat), Lokpa (a thick cloak worn by only women that provides extra warmth), Bok, shawl or Tsa-zar for men.

Shondol dance, which is known as the royal dance of Ladakh, has created history by entering into the Guinness Book of World Records as the largest Ladakhi dance. Shondol is a famous dance, which artistes used to perform for the king of Ladakh

Momos. Arguably the most famous dish in Ladakh, momos are dumplings originating from Tibet which are generally stuffed with minced meat, vegetables (cabbage, potatoes, carrots, onions, spinach) and cheese.

Apricot fruit is known for its high content of Vitamin A and C, calcium, iron, carbohydrates, amino acids, sugar and potassium. For decades the people of Ladakh have consumed the humble apricot, locally known as Chuli.

Chhang is one of the important and indispensable barley based alcoholic beverage prepared and consumed by the people of Ladakh for centuries. Chhang forms a part of sociocultural life and no social activities is complete without the beverage. It quenches thirst, gives energy and provides nutrition.

Mostly in May month the Manali Leh Highway is open for travellers and locals of the region. Currently, only light motor vehicles are allowed, in fact only cars. Heavy vehicles and two-wheelers including bikes are not yet allowed to travel on Manali Leh Highway.

Smiles of Ladakhi tribal man

Broad smile of Ladakhi women

Beautiful landscape of ladakh

Ladakhi Bride in wedding costumes

Traditional wedding jewellery

Buddhist wedding in Ladakh

Wedding ceremony and Buddhist monk

Buddhist bride riding a horse

Ladakhi Couple in wedding dress

Ethnic Jewellery of Ladakh

Native food of Ladakh for weddings

Rituals, Ceremonies and Cultural Heritage of Ladakh's Weddings

Buddhist wedding in Ladakh takes place either in the Buddhist temple or at the bride's home. At home a shrine is erected with a statue of Buddha. The bride and groom light candles and incense and lay flowers around the statue. The 'lama' conducts the wedding.

However a monk may be invited after the marriage ceremony to offer a blessing on the marriage. This will include specific blessings chanted by the monk and maybe a short sermon, probably on marriage.

Marriage has traditionally been viewed as a partnership between the married couple and their families sanctioned by the community and relatives often in a way that shows respect for parents. In many societies where Buddhism is the dominant religion, arranged marriages are the rule.

Most Buddhist ceremonies include a ritual that signifies the joining of husband and wife. Some couples exchange rings in the Western tradition

Nangchangor Chessian refers to the formal engagement ceremony in Buddhist culture. The ceremony is generally presided over by a monk or Rinpoche.

During Buddhist wedding the bride, groom and guests are free to wear whatever they like, as long as it is not too revealing. The bride usually wears a Ladakhi dress and the groom a traditional suit.

A wedding blessing acts as a declaration of approval of the union, especially in cultures where family and community are important. Religious wedding blessings typically appeal to a higher power to watch over the couple and lead them to a long and prosperous marriage.

8. Sikkim

Wedding

Sikkim is North-Eastern state of India.Sikkim is a unique blend of different customs, religion and traditions. Sikkim was occupied by three tribes, Lepchas, Bhutias and Nepalese. Buddhism and Hinduism are the two major religions of Sikkim. Perhaps, Buddhism comes into view as the predominant religious practice in Sikkim. Though, Hinduism is the actual religion that is followed by the majority of people. Buddhism is practiced by most of the Tibetans and the Bhutias.

Sikkim has many hot springs,these hot water springs can be compared to that of a natural spa.There are multiple trekking trails through forests, snowy mountains, and uphill roads.The state is famous for dazzling waterfalls, virgin forests, Tibetan style Buddhist Gompas, alpine meadows, rhododendron flowers and more.

A part of the Eastern Himalaya, Sikkim is notable for its biodiversity, including alpine and subtropical climates, as well as being a host to Kanchenjunga, the highest peak in India and third highest on Earth. Sikkim is bordered by Bhutan, Tibet and Nepal. Part of the Himalayas, the area has a dramatic. Sikkim is also home to glaciers, alpine meadows and thousands of varieties of wildflowers. Steep paths lead to hilltop Buddhist monasteries.Wedding rituals, traditions and ceremonies are entirely different from Southern, Eastern and northern wedding rituals and ceremonies.

Sikkim's Lakes and mountains

Sikkim Wedding is very colorful and loaded with local Traditions

Traditional cloths and customized jewellery for wedding

Gold ornamentstraditional jewellery for Bribe makeup

Traditional wedding dress of Bride and bridegroom

Traditional Sikkim wedding ornaments

Traditional food dishes served during wedding festivals

Historic Traditional Sikkim wedding dance

Rituals, Ceremonies and Cultural Heritage of Sikkim's Weddings

Sikkim, with its rich cultural heritage offers splendid spectacles of unique dressing and celebrations. You can view a fine blend of tradition and contemporary style in Sikkim Weddings. A distinct and charming aura is created in the auspicious occasion of Sikkim Weddings. You can't beat the vibrant celebrations and the magnificence of Sikkim weddings in terms of splendor.

After the horoscopes of the bride and groom are matched, Khachang, a team of four people takes following gifts including a Jaril or Tealeaf, Tsamtruk chi (a basket of puffed rice, a bottle of wine, token cash of Rs. 108 and a long traditional scarf known as hada.

The Saptapadi involves the couple walking seven steps in a clockwise direction around the Angi near the Mandap. Each of the steps is called a 'Phere', and each Phere stands for the seven promises and principles made by the couple to each other during the exchange of vows.

Sikkimese wedding attire is very similar to what their royalty wears and is called a 'bakhu'. A 'bakhu' is made out of the finest silk and is worn in a rather traditional, yet distinct way. It is an ensemble consisting of a loose-fit blouse, a skirt and a belt to tighten at the waistline. The bride wears the royal outfit of Bakhu made in fine silk that is accompanied by a full-sleeved blouse. Beautiful accessories accentuate the wedding look.

As the wedding bells ring in the land of Sikkim, you can see the influence of ethnic as well as modern fashion. Both the bride and the groom wear beautifully designed traditional pure gold jewellery. Small and dignified pieces of jewellery are worn which reflect the simplicity and elegant style. The concept of 'White Weddings' are also becoming very popular in Sikkim. Millions of people staying in Sikkim are adopting this way of the wedding.

Earlier the brides wore wedding gowns in multiple bright and radiant colours. However nowadays, only plain white colour gowns are being opted which appear quite similar to the beautiful wedding gowns of the Christian brides in Sikkim. Gold accessories are now being replaced by very delicate and modern costume jewellery. Brides prefer to wear simple and exquisite jewellery, which matches with the outfits, instead of traditional jewellery. When it comes to accessorizing the wedding look, majority of the couples opt for the purest form of gold jewelry, which weighs nothing less than 24 carats, and is of the most original kind.

The gaiety and spirit of the celebrations during the wedding is really amazing. The Sikkim Wedding involves a number of rituals and formalities. Without those, it cannot get legal sanctity or acceptance by the people of Sikkim. After the horoscopes of the bride and groom are matched, Khachang, a team of four people takes following gifts including a Jaril or Tealeaf, Tsamtruk chi (a basket of puffed rice, a bottle of wine, token cash of Rs. 108 and a long traditional scarf known as hada. After the proposal has been accepted, the groom goes to the bride's maternal uncle to offer "Aaya Seygo" which is a special dish consisting of cooked hen and rice along with soup. Then the date for the Nangchang is fixed. The 'Jo' or a Shamanist priest performs a 'Khelen' ritual with a jar of millet beer and burning incense to signify the marriage tie by invoking the ancestral deities and the family protector deities to shower the blessings. The elderly women assemble in a room in order to finalize Rinzo, which refers to bride's price.

Nyen or marriage is normally conducted in two parts. The first part of the marriage ceremonytakes place at the bride's house. After a period of two years, an auspicious day for the marriage ceremony is fixed by the astrologer. The wedding-feast starts with Chang (millet beer) and sumptuous lunch. In the evening, a group of dancers led by their leader commences the traditional songs in the shrine room, which includes 'Duetse Yarchod' ritual.

The ceremony known as tashi Chanthung is conducted at the groom's house and is called 'Tashi Changthung'.

9. Tamil Wedding

Tamil Nadu, a South Indian state, is famed for its Dravidian-style Hindu temples. The town of Kanyakumari, at India's southernmost tip, is the site of ritual sunrises. Capital Chennai is known for beaches and landmarks including 1644 colonial Fort St. George. This enthralling state is being fascinated with its grand temples, mesmerizing beaches, exotic wildlife and panoramic hill stations. Tamil Nadu is one of India's most well-known traveler destinations owing to its natural splendor. Tamil Nadu is famous for all over the world, it is glorious and ancient temples. Enjoy trekking, surfing and other adventure activities in Tamil Nadu, a state known for its heritage architecture, brilliant sculptures of its ancient temples, performing arts at beaches.

The summer in Tamil Nadu starts in March and ends in May. The temperature may rise up to 40°C, but the hill stations in the state are the best places to visit to escape the heat of plains. Tamil Nadu is much older than North India. It existed as part of the continent called Lemuria that linked Africa and Australia. The Tamils or the Dravidians are therefore one of the earliest races in the world. Prehistoric tools, weapons and burial sites have been discovered in various parts of Tamil Nadu.

Tamil Nadu is the land of festivals and the easiest way to understand the culture of a region is to attend a local festival. Dance Festivals are very famous globally like Nataraj (Dancing Shiva) and Bharat Natyam.

Rich in history, literature and culture, Tamil Nadu is strongly rooted in its heritage. The state has five World Heritage Monument sites certified by UNESCO.

The shining example of Tamil Nadu's legacy is in its architectural heritage. The rock-cut caves to intricately carved temples in the state reflect the skills of the craft people who lived here centuries ago. In Thanjavur, we cannot miss the renowned art and craft that flourishes here which includes the bronze statues.

The temple architecture of South India finds one it's most breathtaking illustrations in the Thanjavur a timeless wonder. The Thanjavur art gallery complex is a major travelers attraction.

Both the destinations comprise of traveller attractions that are filled with natural beauty. Having said that, though both the hill stations offer picturesque views of the mountains, Kodaikanal is rich in fauna due to its forests and Ooty is rich is flora due to its numerous nature parks and gardens.

The heritage-rich state is famous for its ancientculture, colossal temples, alluring rock carvings, intricate silk weaving, and baroque bronze sculptures. The capital of Tamil Nadu is Chennai (Madras) and Tamil is the official language of the state.

Bharat Natyamamazing classic cultural dance

"Thanjavur"a art &culture wonder in Tamil Nadu

Tamil Wedding supporting pretty Kanjivaram Saree

Wedding Excitement and first conversation after wedding rituals

Tamil Bride in her wedding costumes ready for wedding

Tamil bride supporting wedding dress

Togetherness, wedding bliss

Tamil and graceful pretty bride

Smiling Tamil bride after wedding is over

Tamil wedding delicious feast

Maalai or Charam gold &pearls wedding jewellery

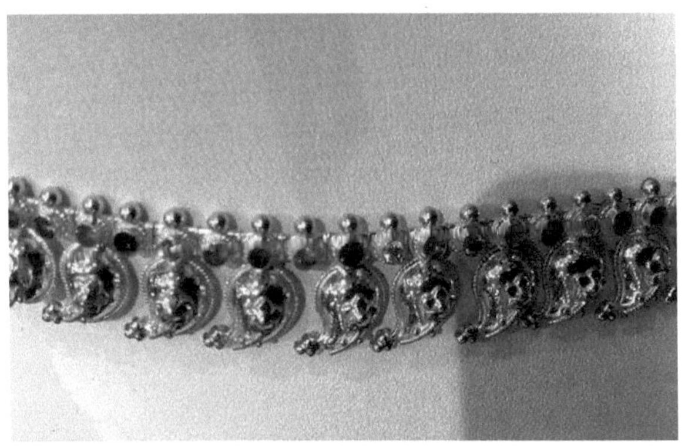

Rituals, Ceremonies and Cultural Heritage of Tamil's Weddings

Typical Tamil weddings are more about sticking to the age old customs and traditions than a lavish affair. For the Tamilians, the spiritual symbolism of a wedding is paramount rather than all the pomp and show. Sure, Tamil weddings are filled with lots of fun and light moments as well as they are a big event with distant relatives in attendance, but there for sure will not be any compromise on the actual ceremony. Tamil weddings, also known as Kalyanam, take place during the day of all months of the Tamilian calendar except Aashad, Bhadrapad and Shunya. It may be expansive if one follows the traditional wedding rituals to a tee, since there are many wedding rituals, without which the marriage will most definitely be deemed incomplete. The important Tamil wedding rituals are given below.

NakshatraPorutham is matching of horoscope are given utmost importance in a Tamil wedding. Horoscopes or nakshatrams are matched following Vedic guidelines based on twelve points or Poruthams like Nadi, Yoni, Rasi, Gana etc. The matching of horoscope determines a lot of factors for the impending wedding like the wedding date, precise moment for the wedding or muhurtha and other rituals as well. Marriage Agreement is drafted next by the priests on both sides once the marriage is fixed. A meeting is arranged at the groom's house where the two sides exchange the marriage agreements by putting it on a platter containing a bunch of bananas, betel leaves, betel nuts and a coconut. Gifts are also exchanged between the families.

Panda Kaal Muhurtham is a ritual which is observed by the bride's and the groom's sides together. The two families visit a temple or may organize a special puja at one of the homes, and pray to the Almighty so that the wedding may happen without any obstacles. This is generally done on the day before the wedding.

Sumangali Prarthanai is a special puja ritual directed towards the Sumangalis or married women who take part during various rituals of the wedding. Generally these women are close relatives and family friends. The women, generally grouped in odd numbers like three or five or seven, gets decked up in traditional nine-yard Madisar sarees. After completion of the puja, the bride seeks blessings from each Sumangali and gives her some special gift like a saree or jewelry. They are also treated with special lunch.

Pallikal Thellichal ritual is when Earthenware pots are decorated with vermillion and sandalwood paste by five or seven married women of the family or both the bride and the groom's families. Inside each pot, nine different types of grains or navadhaanyam are placed along with a bit of curd. A Kolam or traditional south Indian sand art designs that are believed to be bringer of good luck, is prepared at a special spot within the house.

Vrutham is a ritual which takes place at the groom's place on the early mornings of the day before the wedding. The day signifies transition of the groom from the Bachelorhood or Brahmacharya phase of life to Domestic or Garhasthaya phase. He seeks permission from his guru, usually his father to proceed to this phase. A sacred thread, colored yellow with turmeric is tied around the groom's wrists. In a similar ceremony or puja, a yellow thread is also tied around the bride's wrists. This thread is said to protect the bride and the groom from evil energy.

Naandi Shraddham is when groom's family arrives at the bride's place or the venue of the wedding on the morning of the day before. The bride's family welcomes them with tray full of favors like sweets, betel leaves, betel nuts and fruits. The groom is especially welcome with a shower of rose water. A garland is put around the groom's neck and a spot of sandalwood and vermillion paste is applied on his forehead. The bride and his family members are fed sweets prepared by the bride's mother. After the welcome is done, ten Brahmins are invited over who take part in a ritual that offers appeasement to the families' departed ancestors. The Brahmins are treated to traditional Tamil vegetarian lunch and are given traditional two piece garments (veshtiangavastram) along with betel leaves, betel nuts, coconut, fruits and sweets. The Brahmins bless the couple and wish them a prosperous life ahead.

Nishchayathram is the formal engagement ceremony in case of a Tamil wedding. The ritual begins with a puja to lord Ganesh at the bride's home. The groom's family arrives at the bride's house. They gift a beautiful saree to the seated bride and also some jewelry. They then apply a spot of sandalwood paste and vermillion on the bride's forehead. The sumangalis from both sides come and fill up the free end of the bride's saree with rice, fruits, coconut, flower, turmeric, betel nut and betel leaves. An arti (incense and light ritual) of the bride is performed while a floral garland is tied around her waist. The bride's family also performs a similar ritual and gift new clothes to the groom. The bride and the groom then change into these new clothes. If the rituals permit, the couple may exchange rings after they have changed.

Lagna Pathirikai ritual involves announcement of the wedding and offering verbal invitation to the wedding. The family priests after consulting the couple's horoscopes come up with the most auspicious moment of carrying out the wedding which they formally draft in the lagnapatrikai. The lagnapatrikai is supposed to clearly outline the names of the family members, the bride and the groom's, the marriage date and the precise marriage time. This time of the wedding or the Lagna is announced in front of all the family members of both the bride's and the groom's side. The lagnapatrikai is examines and signed by the heads of the two families. Following this gifts are exchanged between the two families.

Traditionally, the Tamil groom wears a two piece garment known as Veshti and Angavastram. Both of these are preferably made of puttu or silk. Veshti refers to the lower part of the garment which the groom wears either like a dhoti or simply by draping it as a lungi. He may wear a simple white shirt or Salvai over it and the angavastram is draped around his neck. He also wears a special headwear known as Thalaip on his head which is sort of like a turban. Nowadays grooms are also partial to Sherwani, Kurtas and other Indo-western outfits like Vests and Jackets. Tamil groom may wear jewelry like gold chains and real or clip on earrings made of gold or diamond.

The Tamil Bride presents a stunning picture of bridal beauty and elegance. Draped in beautiful and traditional Kajeevaram Silk sarees in bright hues paired with gorgeous-looking jewelry, a Tamil Bride is one of the most celebrated icons of the Indian culture. In case of Brahmin brides, the Kanjeevaram sarees are generally 9-yards long while in case of non-Brahmins it is 6-yards. The saree is worn in the traditional Madisar style. The bride's wedding trousseau has to contain more than one of these traditional sarees to be worn at different occasions throughout the course of the celebrations. She wears a separate saree for during the wedding, after the wedding and for the marriage registration ceremony or reception. The sarees are of bright colors with contrasting borders that have gold threads woven into lush designs. She wears her hair in an elaborate plait and bun combination around which flowers are draped in white and orange colors. The Tamil bride wears a lot of jewelry, especially gold ones that are primarily family heirlooms passed through generations. She wears special gold and precious stone set jewelry known as Jadainagam in the shape of a cobra over her plaits, which is believed to be symbolic of the bride's fertility. The ornaments they wear around their waist known as Oddiyanamare made of solid gold with temple designs and is used to keep the saree borders and garlands in place. On her hair, along with the traditional tamilmangtika made of gold, stones and pearls, the Tamil bride also wears special ornaments known as Nethi on both sides of the central hair parting. She generally wears a number of necklaces in multiple layers around her neck, gold bangles, and diamond nosepins.

MangalaSnanam is wedding day which begins at the crack of dawn. The Mangalasnanam ritual is observed separately by the bride and the groom's sides. A paste of turmeric, sandalwood and kumkum is prepared by the Sumangalis or married women. They take turns in applying oil to the bride/groom's hair and massaging the paste on their face, hands and feet. After the ritual, the bride/groom takes a purifying bath in holy water to cleanse their body and soul. They then proceed to get ready for the wedding ceremony.

Gauri is a ritual that is performed by the bride only. An idol of the Goddess Gauri, who represents purity, austerity and virtue, is placed on a plate containing rice and kumkum. She offers her prayers and performs a short puja to the Gauri idol wishing for a happily married life ahead.

Kashi Yathra is ritual when groom's party arrive at the wedding venue and the groom grabs and umbrella, walking sticks and some food items to go off to Varanasi or Kashi, renouncing all worldly attachments to pursue religious studies. The father of the bride then intercepts him outside the wedding hall and makes him see the virtues of the domestic life as opposed to hermit one. The father of the bride then promises the groom to give his daughter to him in marriage. The groom accepts this proposal and returns to the wedding venue to get married. The umbrella is to be kept with the groom throughout the wedding to remind him of the decision and his duties thereby.

Pada Puja when the groom arrives at the wedding mandap, the parents of the bride washes his feet with holy water, sandalwood, milk, and kumkum. His feet are then wiped dry with flower petals.

Maalai Maatral is ritual when bride is then brought into the wedding mandap and the couple exchange flower garlands as a first step of the wedding. The ritual is repeated three times and sometimes amid much playfulness where the bride/groom tries to evade garlanding by the other.

Oonjal refers to a swing. During this ceremony, the couple is made to sit on a swing which is rocked gently. The women of the family surround the swing and sing Oonjal Pattu songs. The elders of the family come one by one and feed the couple milk and banana and bless them. Women from both the families carry colored rice balls around the couple seated in the swing in both clockwise and anticlockwise directions three times before throwing the balls in four cardinal directions to ward off evil energy. Older women also go around the couple holding an earthen lamp and pot filled with water three times in clockwise direction. The gentle rocking motion of the swing represents the turbulent situation that life may present to them.

Kanyadanam when bride and groom is then asked to step off the swing. The end of the bride's saree is tied to the end of groom's angavastram. The bride's mother then applies kajal on the groom's eyes and the bride's father washes his feet. Through this ritual the groom is viewed as representative of Lord Vishnu. The groom is then seated on the floor at his designated spot. The father of the bride sits facing the groom. The bride is seated on her father's lap and a coconut is placed on her hands. The bride's father then supports his daughter's hands and offers the coconut to the groom together. The mother of the bride pours holy water over the coconut. Thus through this formal ceremony, the bride's parents give her to the groom and requests him to take care of their daughter for the rest of their life. The bride and the groom's hands are tied with a sacred thread to seal their union.

Muhurtham is ceremony after completion of the Kanyadanam ritual, the groom's parents presents the bride with a nine yard silk saree symbolizing their acceptance of the bride into their family. The saree is draped around the bride's shoulders while the groom applies vermillion to her hair parting. The bride then goes to change into the saree gifted to her by her in-laws. When she returns to the mandapam, a grass ring is placed on her head, over which the yoke of a plough is placed and a belt made of reed grass is placed around her waist. Water is poured over the yoke. This ritual is symbolic reminder of the fact that the bride and the groom together have to overcome the challenges of life. The Thaali is blessed by the priest and the groom ties the Thaali, or south Indian equivalent of a mangalsutra, around the bride's neck. The first two knots of the Thaali is put in by the groom while the third and the final one is put in by the groom's sister.

Saptapadi when the bride and the groom holds each other's hands and go around the sacred fire seven times. Vedic mantras are chanted by the pries which outlines the seven sacred vows of a marriage. This ritual marks the symbolic beginning of the couple's journey as husband and wife. Next the groom holds the bride's left toe as she steps over a grindstone. This symbolically represents the solidity of their union.

Reception is post wedding ritual when the wedding is followed by a formal reception in the evening where the guests are treated with a lavish vegetarian spread. The newlyweds are seated on thronelike chairs on top of a stage where they can meet and greet all the guests.

Sammandhi Maryathai is post wedding ritual when two families then exchange gifts and the bride prepares to leave her paternal home. She is bid an emotional goodbye by her parents and relatives after they have prayed to the family deity.

Paaladaanam is post wedding ritual isbefore departing of bride. The bride and the groom lie face down and seek the blessings of the elders. The groom then escorts the bride to his home.

Grihapravesham is post wedding ritual when the bride reaches the groom's homeshe is given a warm and celebratory welcome. The mother-in-law performs a small arti and escorts her inside the house where she is led to seek the blessings of the family deity first.

Valeyadal is post wedding ritual refers to the formal introduction of the bride to the members of the groom's family who offers her gifts. Several of the post-wedding games are played to break the ice between the bride and the groom. Maruvidu Varudal is post wedding ritual occur three days after the wedding, the couple visits the bride's paternal home. They are welcomed offered a delicious lunch. The bride's parents gives the couple gifts of clothes as well as jewelry, this mark the end.

10. Amazing

Weddingof Punjab

Rokka (pre-engagement) is one of the most significant ceremonies that take place before a Punjabi wedding. The rokka ceremony marks the union of both the bride and groom's family and friends. Gifts from both families are acceptable at this ritual.

Kurmai (engagement)is important part of a Punjabi wedding. First, the girl is draped with a fulkari (Punjabi craft decorative dupatta "wedding scarf", which is usually ornate. In some families this chunni (Scarf) is a family heirloom, passed down from generation to generation. She is also presented with jewellery ornaments, which her mother and sister-in-law help her wear. Pretty tiny dot of henna paste is applied to her palm for good luck, and the function is closed with the exchange of rings. The bride's father applies the tikka (religious forehead mark) to the groom's forehead and blesses him. Exchange of gifts takes place between the two families. Everyone present congratulates the couple by feeding them sweets.

Dholki(traditional musical drum)and sangeet(wedding Songs) function hosted by the bride's family, in which just a few close members of the groom's family are invited. The bride's family plays the dholak(drums)and sing songs in which they tease the groom and his family. Nowadays, people hire DJs and have a dance party, followed by dinner. A ladies sangeet *and* cocktail is held for the bride and her bridesmaids.

Mehndi(Henna) is unique artistic wedding tradition the last major function before the wedding is decoration with temporary henna (mehndi) tattoos. This is often blended with the sangeet ceremony. Mehndi artists are called to the houses of the boy and girl and apply mehndi to the palms ofthe female family members, groom and the hands and feet of the bride.

A basket containing BindiForehead mark) (and bangles is handed around so girls can choose those that match the outfit they plan to wear to the wedding. The Mehndi ceremony takes place in the atmosphere of a party. The bride and other ladies get mehndi (henna designs) done, on their hands and feet (most ladies get it done only on their hands but the bride gets it done on both hands and feet). For the bride the mehndi is sent by the future Mother in Law, which is beautifully decorated.

Choora (set of wedding original red bangles made from elephant teeth) is ritual at bride home. On the wedding day the rituals at the girl's home begin with the Choora ceremony. The oldest maternal uncle and aunt play an important role in the performance of the ceremony. Choora is basically a set of Red bangles, gifted by girl's mama (mother's brother). People touch the choora and give their heartiest wishes to the girl for her future married life. Also, they sprinkle flower petals on the bride. After that, the girl's uncle, aunt, friends and cousins tie kaliras (silver, gold or gold plated traditional ornaments) to a bangle worn by the girl.

Mayian (Turmeric) is the preparation ceremony one day before a Punjabi wedding. This ceremony is an evening festival, at the couple's parental homes. It consists of many rites, the Batna (cleanse the skin and create a glow), Choora(wedding bangles), Jaggo (night awakening ceremony), fireworks and sometimes the Ladies Sangeet (songs) and Mehndi Heena). The mayian happens the night before the wedding and is celebrated according to which part of Punjab the participants are from

During Vatna (traditional ceremony taking place a few days prior to your wedding) ceremonyfour lamps or diyas (clay lamps) are lit and the bride sits facing them. Oil is constantly poured into the lamps, so that the glow from the diyas is reflected on her face. Vatna involves applying a paste made from turmeric powder and mustard oil all over the bride's body by her female friends and relatives. This is done to make the bride look more beautiful on the most special day of her life. This ritual demands that the bride stay at home in her old clothes for a couple of days before her wedding.

Ubtan is supposed to bring a glow to the bride's and groom's body, especially on their faces. This tradition is also known as Shaint in some cultures. After this ritual, the bride and groom are constrained from meeting each other until the wedding ceremony.

Ghara gharoli ceremony is a decorated pitcher of water (ghadoli) is brought for the bride's bath by the bride's bhabi (brother's wife). In the ghara gharoli ritual, the bride's sibling or sibling's spouse visits the nearby temple and fills a pitcher with holy water. The girl is then bathed with this holy water. Thereafter, the bride wears her wedding attire. The ghara gharoli and the vatna ceremonies take place at the groom's house too. But over there, the groom's sister-in-law brings the pitcher of water. As per the tradition, their wedding dress is presented to them by their respective maternal uncles.

Jaggo (Keep Awake) In this ceremony, the family dances and sings in the beautifully decorated wedding home. Jaggo is celebrated in the last hours of the night. They decorate copper or brass vessel called khadaa with diveh (clay lamps) and fill them with mustard oil and light them. The bride or bridegroom's maternal aunt (mami) carries it on her head, and another woman will carry a long stick with bells, shaking it. The women will then go into other friends' and families' homes; after being welcomed by sweets and drinks, they dance there and move on. It is a loud ceremony, filled with joy, dancing, fireworks, and food.

Sarvala (Best man) rituals take place at groom's home where a young nephew or cousin dons the same attire as the groom. He is called the sarvala (caretaker of the groom) and accompanies him.

Sehra is ritual where groom riding a decorated wedding horse with sarala (Best Man). Like the bride's home, the Vatna and Ghara Gharoli are followed by the dressing up of the groom in his wedding attire. After the groom has dressed up in his wedding clothes, a puja is performed. Thereafter, the groom's sister ties the sehra on the groom's head. After the completion of Sehrabandi (Groom wedding turban)ceremony, all those who witness the function give gifts and cash to the boy as a token of good luck.

A groom support sehra(Wedding turban) during sehra ceremony. Varna is a ceremony that is supposed to ward off the evil eye. The groom's bhabi (sister-in-law) lines his eyes with surma (kohl). Ghodi Chadna (Mare riding) is the final ceremony at the groom's place. The groom's sisters and cousins feed and adorn his mare. To ward off the evil eye, people use cash and perform the Varna (ward off the evil eye using Kohl) ritual. The cash is then distributed among the poor. After this the boy climbs the horse and leaves his home for the wedding venue

Ghodi chadna (mare ridding) rituals at the marriage venueIn the ceremony, the groom sets off for the wedding venue by riding a horse. The horse is decorated well and a tika is applied on its head and is fed chana dal(lentils) by the ladies of the groom's family. The Surma is applied to the groom's eyes by his sister-in-law to protect him from evil eyes.

Milni literally means "introductions". In a Sikh marriage, Ardas (religious reading) is performed by the person in charge of looking after the Sikh scriptures, followed by the formal introductions of senior men in the families. For example, both eldest chachas (father's younger brother) will come together and exchange garlands of flowers. In the Milni ceremony, the girl's relatives give shagun (a token of good luck) to the groom's close relatives in descending order of age. Cash and clothes are gifted.

After Milini bride and groom come in the center of the circle where the family is standing, and place a heavily made garland made of flowers- Jaimala (flowers garland) on each other to state, they accept each other and will love and live together with one another. Friends and relatives of the bride and groom indulge in teasing and fun, to celebrate this happy occasion. An auspicious time or "muhurat" is chosen for the performance of wedding ceremony.

Kanyadaan (ceremony to give daughter) and Phere (Wedding Circles) is next ritual. The bride's father puts a ring on the boy's finger and then he gives his daughter to the boy. This ritual is known as the Kanyadaan. It is after the kanyadaan that the pheras begin. The pheras take place in front of the sacred fire, agni (Holy fire).

After this the groom applies Sindoor (vermilion) to the girl's hair partition and the Mangalsutra Rasam (bride necklacerituals) takes place where the groom ties a beaded necklace i.e. a mangalsutra to the girl's neck. When all these rituals are over, the couple gets up to touch the feet of all the elder members in the family and seek their blessings for a happily married life. In a Hindu Punjabi Wedding, Agni (sacred fire) is usually encircled four times.

In a Sikh wedding, the bride and groom will walk in tow around the holy book of Sikh religion four times, called laavaan (rounds)at Sikh Anand Karaj. This signifies they not only vow to see each other as one soul in two bodies, the ideal in Sikh marriage, but also as the Guru as the center of their marriage. Sikhs do not do pujas during any part of the marriage ceremony.

Joota chupai literally means 'hiding the shoes'. The bride's sisters indulge in stealing of shoes. It is a fun tradition, in which the girls charge a fee for agreeing to return the shoes. They demand Kalecharis of gold for the bride's sisters and of silver for her cousins.

Ring finding ritual is post-wedding rituals in this Punjabi wedding game a bowl full of milk, rose petals and a few other objects are placed. The couple's wedding rings are then immersed into the bowl. They then try finding their ring using only one hand. The partner that first finds the ring is said to have the upper hand in the marriage.

Vidaai Doli is post-wedding rituals marks the departure of the bride from her parental house, which marked as sad events on bride side. As a custom, the bride throws phulian (roasted rice) or puffed rice over her head. The ritual conveys her good wishes for her parents.

A traditionally sad ritual, here the bride says goodbye to her parents, siblings and rest of her family. Her brothers/male cousins then lead her to her husband, who waits to take her to his family home to begin her new life as a married woman. Her relatives throw coins in the wake of this procession. In keeping with tradition the mother in-law will often not come to the Doli and instead make preparations at home to greet the arrival of her son and new wife.

The mother-in-law has a glass of water in her hand, which she circles 3 times around her bahu (daughter-in-law) and then offers it to her to drink, as a symbol of her acceptance and blessing as her newest daughter.

Reception,rituals observed at the groom's house. The newlyweds are welcomed in a ceremony called the pani bharna (water filling). Then the bride must, with her right foot, kick the "sarson ka tel" (mustard oil) that is put on the sides of the entrance door before she enters the house.

Then couple offer puja in their room. Touch the feet of the elders in a ceremony called "matha tekna" (Four head bowing). The newly-wedsvisit the bride's parents on the day after the wedding. The bride's brother usually fetches them and this ceremony called Phera Dalna (Visitation).

Vibrant Gidha dance by Punjabi damsels

Couple exchange gifts after wedding

Bride of Punjab decked will jewellery for wedding

Couple exchange wedding Complimentary

Bride dressed in traditional Punjabi style

Modern style Punjabi wedding

"Chunni" (Scarf) ritual relatives of bride accompany her

Punjabi groom wedding with British bride

Bride dressed up with gold jewellery for wedding

Bride dressed up in Punjabi costumes

Traditional drum musicPunjabi wedding

Hilarious Punjabi bride with wedding gown

Married Punjabi couple with tradition sword custom

Jaggo ceremony during wedding at night time

Wedding feast during wedding in Punjab

Rituals, Ceremonies and Cultural Heritage of Punjab's Weddings

Punjab, a state bordering Pakistan, is the heart of India's Sikh community aswell Hindis. The city of Amritsar, founded in the 1570s by Sikh Guru Ram Das, is the site of Harmandir Sahib, the holiest gurdwara (Sikh place of worship). Known in English as the Golden Temple, and surrounded by the Pool of Nectar, it's a major pilgrimage site. Also in Amritsar is Durgiana Temple, a Hindu shrine famed for its engraved silver doors.

This fertile land ranks amongst the most ancient civilizations in the world. Punjab is also famous for its religious diversity as it was here many religious movements were initiated. The scenic landscape, rich history and famous religious sites are the most important reasons for increasing number of visits by tourists.

Punjab has always been land of great saints and fighters. Tourist places - Punjab is the place of Sikhism. The holiest of Sikh shrines, the Sri Harmandir Sahib (or Golden Temple), is in the city of Amritsar. The five Takhts (Temporal Seats of religious authority) of Sikhism, three are in Punjab.

Butter Chicken, king of all Punjabi dishes is so delicious. Shakkar Para, a sweet and indulgent dish of Punjab. Lassi (Butter milk), Chole (Lentils), Bhature(Oiled baked thick chapatti) is Punjabi Food Fiesta. Parantha (wheat baked chappti) is the Staple Food of Punjab, Amritsari Fish,non-veggie delights, Dal Makhani (Butter lentils) and saeso ka saag (Mustard leave puree).

Phulkari(traditional Panjabi dress) dress is very gorgeous traditional handicraft of Punjab. If you look out for a Punjabi woman's wardrobe, you will always find a Phulkari Dupatta (scarf) there. Embroidered with intricate thread work on different fabrics like: cotton, raw silk, or georgette, these dupattas (Scraf) are often worn on special occasions adding a charm to the beauty of women.

Punjabi people are very fond of meeting and greeting people with a lot of love and affection. With their gestures, they would make you feel as if they have known you for years. Of course, they don't dance their way to strangers but they are quite good at making instant connections with new people they meet.

Like most of us, Punjabis, too, have a sedentary lifestyle and one cannot digest all that ghee as our ancestors did. They used to do a lot of manual work. Hence they were able to burn these calories effectively.

Punjabis are big-time food lovers, preferring a wide variety in their menu. They are full of life and their food too reflects this liveliness. Punjabi food forms an important part of the North Indian cuisine, which appeals to the taste of many.

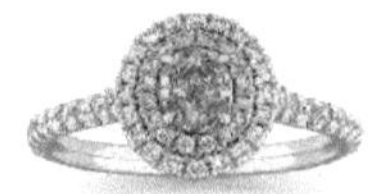

11. Wedding'sthrill

In tribal Nagaland

Nagaland unique heritage sites, rich wildlife, local festivals, delicious cuisines, beautiful handicrafts, cultural shopping, attractive places, attractions and more. Nagaland State is replete with festivities throughout the year, as all tribes celebrate their own festivals with a pageantry of colour, music and dance. A common feature is that the festivals revolve around agriculture, the mainstay of Naga economy. These festivals hark back to times prior to the advent of Christianity.

Nagaland is a mountainous state in northeast India, bordering Myanmar. It's home to diverse indigenous tribes, with festivals and culture celebrating the different tribes' tradition. The Nagaland State Museum exhibits ancient weaponry, a ceremonial drum and other traditional Naga cultural artifacts.

Nagaland is amongst the smallest state in India. Endowed with abundant natural beauty of mountains and mesmerizing hills makes for the spell-binding vistas that are considered to be the major attractions of Nagaland.

It is also popularly known as the 'land of festivals and every tribal festival is celebrated with pomp and gaiety, adorned with rich and colorful traditional attires. The most vibrant being the 'Hornbill Festival' where the songs of the ancient Nagas echo and its music reverberates in the true spirit of the tribal men.

Naga Tribal Girl from remote hamlet

Nagaland Capital beautiful skyline

Naga bride dressed for wedding

Hilarious Couple after wedding ceremony

Naga bride traditionally dressed

Married couple celebrating honeymoon with nature

Naga wedding feast with delicious food

Tribal wedding of Naga with traditional dress

Tribal bridal necklace of Nagas

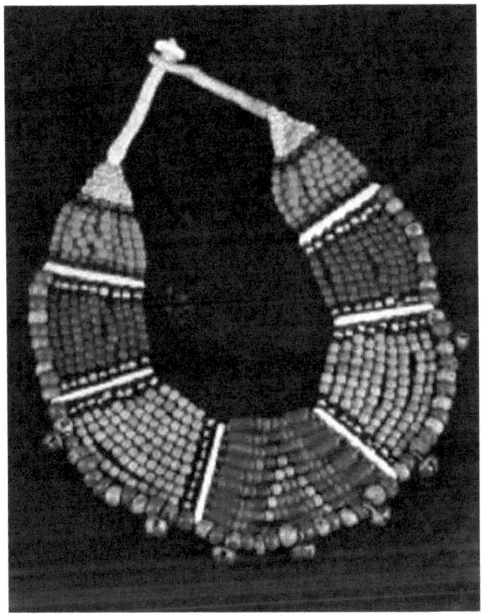

Rituals, Ceremonies and Cultural Heritage of Nagaland's Weddings

Nagaland has 16 different tribes. The Ao tribe is one such tribe. When the groom decides to get engaged to a girl of his choice, Ao Naga (Groom/eligible bachelor) usually offers fish to the bride's parents. They also sacrifice fowls in most phases of the wedding.

The Naga tribes of Nagaland follow the exogamous principles for weddings. People of the same clan do not marry each other. The only exception in this case is the Konyak chiefs. They are considered sacred and their wives can be of the same clan

Traditional Wedding Ceremony Order are as following: The processional begins with bridesmaids and groomsmen walking down the aisle, typically paired up. Second,words of welcome and thanks. Once everyone is in place, the officiant will say a few words of welcome.

Next session is introduction and text reading.A few people may be invited up to share or exchange readings at this point in the ceremony. Then Officiant addressescouple. Exchange Vows, Ring Exchange. Concludingfinal kiss ceremony.

When the groom decides to get engaged to a girl of his choice, Ao Naga (Groom/eligible bachelor) usually offers fish to the bride's parents. They also sacrifice fowls in most phases of the wedding. The leilenga ceremony takes place on the wedding day. The bride makes the wedding garlands for herself and her partner.

The Officiant, Groom, Best Man, and Groomsmen enter first, typically from the side of the ceremony site but sometimes up the aisle depending on preference. Following them are the grandparents, the parents of the Groom, and the Mother of the Bride. Finally, the Bridesmaids, Maid of Honor, and Flower Girl enter.

A wedding reception is a party usually held after the completion of a marriage ceremony as hospitality for those who have attended the wedding, hence the name reception, the couple receive society, in the form of family and friends, for the first time as a married couple.

Did you ever get a chance to attend Nagaland Wedding? No, let's explore its rituals. Usually, the Naga's follow strict and exogamic custom of marriage. Physical intimacy is completely prohibited between them. Only the people from Konyak tribe are inviolable, who believe in bringing wife from the same clan. There is a small story about the birth of the sacred tribes. Nikhoga, who was the first man of the Naga tribes had six sons. He found a wife only for his eldest son. An interest and fascination were created amongst all the brothers. Nikhoga was disgusted with this feeling and threw all the other 5 sons' out of his house, who in turn formed the sacred tribes.

In Angamis tribes, a young lad chooses a girl and demands to marry her, to his father, who in turn sends his friend to get an approval to the girl's parents. On mutual agreement, the groom's father tests the bride. A fowl is strangled to death, observing how it crosses the legs while dying. If the legs are crossed in unfavorable conditions, the wedding is broken off. If in the next 3 days, the to-be-bride dreams something inappropriate, the wedding is called off. If all goes well, the wedding is finally fixed.

The rituals begins at the bride's house with a feast and by evening she proceeds to her husband's home. Staying in the same house, the couple is not allowed to sleep together, they visit the field on the 3rd day but night separates the duo. The priest of the village calls the couple on the 8th or 9th daythat is when they are allowed for a sexual intimacy.

Amongst the Mongsen Tribe Once the boy and the girl are engaged, they go for a 20-days trading business tour. Without profits in the tour, the engagement is not successful. It is considered a bad sign. Earning profits in business is a good sign, and the wedding is proceeded.

The Naga women are very strong and they always keep themselves busy in different fields as per their interest. The girls are pretty, fair, good body dignity but short, their heads are shaved when they reach the marriageable age. This is done so that the girls do not fall for any boy and do not commit any unacceptable act.

In Sema's Tribe, the girls are kept very carefully; the reason is that a very high price is offered to them for marriages. The amount is reduced if a girl is caught in any inevitable act. The opposite side in this condition has to pay huge fine. The amount depends on the position, the girl's father hold in the society, and also on the decided amount of the girl's marriage. Earlier, as the girls reach their teens, were made to sleep in a different house amongst a group of other girls.

Nagaland Weddings presently are no less than any other Indian Weddings. They have also started following the showbiz system. A huge amount is spent on the decor, the brides and grooms' dresses.

Moreover, the Nagaland Weddings have become a hybrid affair mix of their old wedding traditions and a bit picked from powerful influence of these days expensive weddings.

12. Hyderabad

Wedding

Hyderabad is the capital of southern India's Telangana state. A major center for information technology industry,Hyderabad is a city with a rich royal heritage. Hyderabad is a city with a rich royal heritage. While many of the ancient traditions have been updated, the grandeur has not been lost! It is also called 'The City of Kings,' Hyderabad has many traditions unique to its own cultural heritage, and a traditional

Hyderabad has many traditions unique to its own cultural heritage, a former diamond-trading center.From historical monuments to natural getaways to mouth-watering world famous cuisine and thrilling entertainment parks.

Wonderla Amusement and Waterpark is undoubtedly a place of unlimited fun and boundless entertainment. Wonderla has been maintaining international standards of facilities along with an extensive array of dry and water rides and games.

Traveler magazine of National Geographic ranked Hyderabad as the Second best place in the world to visit in 2015. Hyderabad is a delightful blend of traditional pearl shops, authentic flavours Irani cafes, lavishness of Taj

Falaknuma Palace, liveliness of decades old Laad Bazaar, the aromas of Hyderabadi cuisine and much more. Experience its enchanting historical touch which has been weaved artistically in the thread of its modern living.

Wedding ceremony & family get togather

Ritual bride garlanded by groom

Bride ready for wedding rituals

Bride ready to meet her life partner

Fun and frolic with wedding dance

Romantic conversation after wedding in couple

Hyderabad delicious Wedding feast

Rituals, Ceremonies and Cultural Heritage of Hyderabad's Weddings

Mangini (Engagement) is pre-wedding ceremony with all weddings, Hyderabad Muslim traditions also begin with a Mangini or engagement. This is the official betrothal ceremony and the date of the wedding is sometimes fixed during this occasion. While this is not a major ceremony in most household, some do arrange a small party on the day.

Mehendi (Henna) pre-wedding ceremony one of the most significant among Hyderabad Muslim traditions is the Mehendi. This is a ladies role where they either hire someone to come home and apply it on all the ladies and bride hands or they go to a Mehendi specialist's home. Everybody who is female gets their hands blemished, little girls included.

Manjha (Turmeric) pre-wedding ceremony is like to the 'Haldi' (turmeric) ceremony in other parts of India, where turmeric is made into a paste with sandalwood or saffron and apply to the bride's skin. A token quantity of paste is also applied to the groom. The paste for the bride generally arrives from the groom's house and unmarried girls take turns to apply it to the bride to make her glow for her special day. Traditionally, once the Manjha is completed with, the bride is not believed to leave her house until the wedding day.

Baraat (groom wedding team)is wedding day where the groom is generally dressed in a Sherwani, the fabric of which is usually something heavy like brocade. He also has a turban to match the Sherwani, and it is generally decorated with a jewel of some kind. The groom sits on a white mare and is accompanied by his relations to the bride's home, amidst much singing and dancing.

Entry of the bride is on wedding day bride dress in a traditional Khada Dupatta set, which include a kurta or tunic, tight pants (Chudidaar) or a long divided skirt (Gharara) and a long flowy dupatta or shawl that is draped around her. An ornate veil is then placed on her head which flows down her back. Muslim brides often wear heavy gold jewelry, most of which have been passed down several generations. She is brought into the wedding hall accompanied by her relatives (usually siblings) who hold a decorative shawl over her head.

Nikaah is Hyderabad Muslim Traditions usually dictate a segregation of some sort, although modern weddings see less and less of it. Traditionally, the men are grouped together around the priest, the groom, and the bride's father, while the womenfolk sit with the bride at a distance or on another floor. The marriage is made official and legal by the priest and the bride signs on the Nikah or marriage agreement, after giving her consent by saying 'Qubool hai.

Arsi Musaf is a unique wedding tradition that is quite sweet too! After the Nikah, the groom goes to sit next to the bride. Their heads are covered with a veil and both of them are asked to read passages from the Holy Quran. They are then asked to look into a mirror, where they see their reflection for the first time as man and wife. At this point, they usually share a sweetened drink of some sort and are fed dates by the elders to convey their blessings.

Walima (celebration of marriage) a post about Hyderabad Muslim traditions cannot be complete without any mention of food. Of course, the famed Hyderabad Biriyani(delicious fried rice) is the center of attraction, but there are several other dishes that are just as delicious. The dinner usually begins with Haleem(stew composed of meat, lentil and pounded wheat made into a thick paste) andalso includes Red Chicken, Luqmi(a typical mince savoury or starter of the cuisine of Hyderabad), Kabab(Indian spices mixed with minced meat), Vegetable Pulao (fried rice), and many dishes, most of which feature mutton or mince. Desserts are rich affairs made with milk, cream, and dry fruits.

Rukhsati (Departure)is the tradition where the husband takes his new wife to her marital home. In the older days, when the groom and his relatives were from a distant village, the groom stayed at the bride's home on the wedding night, but in another room. The Rukhsati was then held the next morning, amid tears and chirpy farewells.Also during wedding feast time some fragrant Hyderabad Biryani visible at each wedding. While Hyderabad Muslim traditions may vary from house to house, the dinner or Daawat(invitation) is something no one compromises on. So the next time you get an invite for a Hyderabad Muslim Marriage, prepare to get your hearts and tummies filled.

13. Wedding in Goa

Goa is very famous for beaches and also for fabulous beach wedding ceremonies. Goa is a state in western India with coastlines stretching along the Arabian Sea. Its long history as a Portuguese colony prior is evident in its preserved 17th-century churches and the area's tropical spice plantations. Goa is also known for its beaches, ranging from popular stretches at Baga and Palolem to those in laid-back fishing villages.

Travellers visiting Goa for leisure, wellness purposes, typically for a short duration and staying at various accommodation units in Goa.

Goa is a famous tourist spot for Indians because of its dazzling nightlife that never ends. This city offers amazing, and exciting nightlife that starts from nightclubs, bars, beach shacks, and more with non-stop music, latest songs, perfect ambiance, dizzy neon lights, delectable food, and fancy drinks.

Pork vindalooisderived from the Portuguese words for garlic(alho) and wine (vinho), combined in a marinade, this spicy Goan curry originated from a Portuguese sailor's dish made with - yes, that's right - pork, garlic and wine. Crab xec-xec. Prawn balchao,

Sanna, Goan red rice. Chouris pao, Poee, Kingfish, Pineapple, banana, papaya, chiku (Mud apple), durian, passion fruit, as well as grapes, watermelons, melons, and figs are available fresh throughout the year. Mango, a favorite, is available in the summer.

Fabulous Beach wedding Goa

Beach wedding at night time

Christian wedding in Goa

Wedding armaments beside beach in Goa

Bride of affluent family, Goa wedding

Grace and Charm of Traditional wedding

Goa bride and groom after wedding

Wedding delicious feast of Goa

Rituals, Ceremonies and Cultural Heritage of Goa's Weddings

The agreement between the two parties must be free and voluntary and without compulsion, undue influence, or threat of violence. The marriage must be witnessed by two reliable eye-witnesses and by a licensed marriage performer.

Pre-wedding events are part of the excitement of getting married. They provide a chance to gather with close friends and family members to share your joy, reminisce and plan for the future. Pre-wedding parties include everything from the engagement party to the rehearsal dinner.

The mother of the bride plays the role of hostess, meaning you should spend some time greeting guests during the reception. Although there are exceptions, other wedding-day duties may include sitting at the parents' table and dancing with the father of the bride to help warm up the dance floor.

It is also announced in their respective churches. It is also announced in their respective churches. Bridal Shower: It is an event held for the bride and just female guests are invited. Bachelor or Bachelorette Party: The Roce Ceremony, Bridal Entrance and Exchange of Vows. “I do”, the bouquet toss andreception. Bridal shower is an event held for the bride and just female guests are invited

An Indian Christian wedding often has the haldi and mehendi ceremony. Both bride and groom at their respective houses are applied haldi amidst dance and music. Mehendi takes place at the residence of the bride, usually a day before the wedding. This ceremony is also accompanied by music and dance.

Officiant stands at the altar. Groom and best man enter from a side door and stand at the altar. Bridesmaids and ushers walk in pairs (if there are uneven numbers, the odd person can walk alone, or two maids or groomsmen can walk together). The maid or matron of honor walks alone.

The bride and groom are the first to exit during the recessional. They are then followed by the flower girl and the ring bearer. The maid of honor and best man will then make their way down the aisle, followed by the remaining bridesmaids and groomsmen. The bride and groom's parents will then exit.

The maid of honor usually stands closest to the bride and holds the bride's bouquet. If one of your besties is a matron of honor, you can ask her to stand in the second spot.

This expense is traditionally covered by the bride's family since they often host the engagement party at their house as a way to welcome and bring together the two families (usually for the first time!). However, whichever family is feeling the most generous can offer to host or throw the engagement party.

Since the bride's family pays for the engagement party, the rehearsal dinner is traditionally paid for by the groom's parents. They should only spend what they're comfortable with, however, and hosting a small soirée the day before the wedding is more than enough.

The wedding rings are a split cost between the bride and groom's families. The groom's family pays for the bride's ring and vice versa.

The bouquet should be a gift from the groom to the bride. For an extra romantic twist, the groom could even pick wildflowers for the bride's bouquet. On the other hand, the bride's side of the family will traditionally pay for all floral decorations. Check out this article if you're not sure how to choose your wedding flowers.

The bride's side of the family traditionally pays for the bride's wedding dress and the bridesmaids' dresses. Increasingly, however, bridesmaids are paying for their own dresses. It really depends on what your budget is, the type of dresses you want your bridesmaids to wear, and whether or not that's within their price range! To avoid confusion later, we'd recommend discussing this as early as possible with your wedding squad.

Check out our ultimate list of the best places to get bridesmaid dresses. As for suits for the best man and the ushers. Unless they'll be matching or require special suits, the ushers should pay for them themselves. If the suits need to be tailor-made, however, it's an expense that the groom's side should cover.

Traditionally, each side of the family pays for their own guests' accommodation. However, this really depends on what the families are comfortable with and most guests pay for their own accommodation nowadays. Just make sure you mention this on your information sheet!

Traditionally, it's the groom who pays for the honeymoon. Today, however, most couples split the cost, with many also asking for donations towards their honeymoon instead of wedding gifts. This is a relatively new traditionlikely stems from the fact that people are getting married later and often already live together by the time they tie the knot.

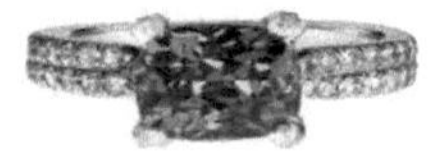

14. Wedding from Orissa

Orissa or Odisha (as it is called now) is state of great biodiversity, abundance of nature, architecturally marvelous temples and simplicity.

Odisha, the eastern coast of Indian state is well-known to world forenrich traditions and culture. Odisha is gaining recognition as a pilgrimage destination.

Today Odisha becomes one of the key cosmopolitan centers of eastern India. Odisha tour package includes Culture, Art, Craft, and Tradition, Festival along with sightseeing let you experience the life of Odisha.

Odisha includes wide range of culture not only to see and learn new things in Odisha but also enjoy mingling with natural and diversified beauty of state of India. Odisha offer to watch amazing Tribal people, Wildlife, ancient temples and Buddhist places,

The marriage happens in three major rituals, Nirbandha (fixing the marriage), Bahaghara (wedding) and Chauthi (consummation). A marriage is not considered complete or valid until consummation.

These rituals are performed either at the Duara (bride's house) or Tola kanias house (the bridegroom's residence).Bahaghara (Odia also called as Odia Hindu wedding) is a wedding ceremony performed by Odia Hindu people in the Indian state of Odisha. There are subtle differences in the rites observed by different castes. In Odia marriage rituals, the mother of the bridegroom does not take part in the ceremony.

The marriage happens in three major rituals, Nirbandha (fixing the marriage), Bahaghara (wedding) and Chauthi (Chaturthi) (consummation). A marriage is not considered complete or valid until consummation.

These rituals are performed either at the Duara (bride's house) or Tola kanias house (the bridegroom's residence). Bahaghara (Odia also called as Odia Hindu wedding) is a wedding ceremony performed by Odia Hindu people in the Indian state of Odisha. There are subtle differences in the rites observed by different castes. In Odia marriage rituals, the mother of the bridegroom does not take part in the ceremony.

One of the main food dishes of Orissa/ Odisha, Santula is a classic Oriya delicacy that you can slurp and slurp even more on your trip. Made with raw papaya, brinjal, and tomato, the dish has more greens and fewer spices, thereby having all the makings for a healthy dish.

Chhena jalebi is the Odia version of the famous North Indian sweet. The only difference in both the variants is that Odisha's jalebi is made using cottage cheese and therefore has a soft texture compared to the traditional jalebi.

Beautiful beaches of Orissa

Orissa is famous for traditional dance

A Bride from Orissa dressed up for Wedding Occasion

Bride with wedding pride and charming smile

Orissa traditional Food for Wedding

Newly Wedof Orissa in traditional dress

Traditional Dress and dance

Traditional Wedding in Orissa

Rituals, Ceremonies and Cultural Heritage of Orissa's Weddings

Orissa (Odiya) weddings are very simple just like the people of the state. Minimalism is one word that describes Oriya weddings at its best. Let's have a look at various rituals, customs, etc., associated with Odiya weddings. The simplicity of Oriya people is reflected in their wedding customs as well. They are devoid of any ostentatious display of wealth and status. They place a lot of importance on traditional customs and adherence to their roots. The wedding rituals are according to Vedic Hindu rituals that have been modified with layers of regional and cultural practices. Religious devotion plays an important role in the life of Oriya people and it is reflected in their wedding customs. The Oriya word for wedding is Bahaghara

Nirbandh is pre-wedding rituals. Most Oriya families prefer arranged marriage for their children. Matches are searched through a matchmaker or within the community. Inter-community matches are not very encouraged among Oriya families. Once a suitable match is found, there is horoscope matching. If the horoscope matches satisfactorily, then the two families meet. After this meeting, if the families feel that all is well, they set a date for the Nirbandh, or the formal engagement ceremony. During an Oriya engagement ceremony, the bride and groom are generally not present. It is the elders of the family who meet at the bride's home or at a temple and give each other their words or Sankalpa that they will marry their children. The ritual is also known as Vak Nischaya, or word of mouth. Both the families exchange some gifts.

Jayee Anukolo is a pre-wedding ritual. The Jayee Anukolo ceremony marks the beginning of the wedding ceremony. Wedding cards are ordered by the families and their distribution marks the formal announcement of the wedding to the community. The first invitation card is placed before Lord Jagannath, the supreme deity for Oriya people, preferably at his main temple at Puri. This ritual is known as Deva Nimantrana. The second invitation is generally sent to the maternal uncle's families, for both the bride's and the groom's sides. A member of the family visits personally and presents the invitation card with a betel leaf and betel nut. This custom is known as Moula Nimantrana. The third invitation goes from the bride's family to the groom's family. The bride's father, accompanied by other male family members, visits the groom's house with the invitation and gifts and personally invites the groom. This custom is known as Jwain Nimantrana. The families are now free to distribute the invitation cards to other relatives, friends and acquaintances.

Mangan is pre-wedding rituals. On the afternoon of the day before the wedding, the bride and groom undergo a ritual that is the Oriya equivalent of Haldi. Turmeric is made into a paste and the paste is applied on the bride/groom's hands and feet by seven married women, one of which must be the sister-in-law. The bride and groom are then bathed with holy water.

Jairagodo Anukolo is a pre-wedding ritual. This ceremony marks the lighting of a holy flame that is considered auspicious for the upcoming wedding. The fire is lit either in form of an oil or ghee lamp, or in the form of a havan. It has to be kept lit till all the wedding rituals are completed.

Diya Mangula Puja is pre-wedding rituals. This ritual involves offering of prayers and conducting a puja at the local temple, most commonly of the village goddess or gramadevati. The bride's wedding saree, toe rings, bangles and a container of vermillion is offered to the Goddess and her blessings are sought. This ritual is generally done through the local barber's wife. It is believed that the Goddess' blessings on these objects will result in a long and happy married life.

Nandimukha ispre-wedding rituals. At both the bride's and the groom's place a ritual called Nandimukha is observed where the respective fathers pray to the ancestors to shower their blessings on the couple.

Traditional bridegroom attires are mostly self-made. Traditionally, the Oriya men prefer wearing Dhoti during the wedding ceremony. These may be simple cotton ones or may be made of silk. Modest dhotis have a simple and demure border with a white base, while modern-day grooms may prefer to wear dhotis in various other colors and with more elaborate borders. Over the Dhoti the groom wears a Cotton Shirt or a kurta typically worn by men in most eastern states. He also wears some form of ethnic slippers with the outfit. He is made to wear a colorful and glittering crown made of Shola or Cork Pith.

The bride is traditionally adorned in a yellow saree with red border known as Boula Patta. However, modern-day Oriya brides prefer wearing elaborate sarees like benarasi or kanjeevaram or even local Ikkat silk sarees in red or similar colors that have some sort of ornate embroidery with zari or sequin work. She pairs the saree with an ornate brocade blouse. Another compulsory part of the Oriya bride's wedding attire is the Dupatta or the Uttariyo. The bride covers her head with the Dupatta which is adorned with zari and sequins as well. Like the groom, the bride wears a matching headwear. She generally wears aesthetically pleasing jewelry, preferably made of gold, including necklace, earrings, bangles and rings.

Barjaatri a is wedding day ritual. The groom sets off from his home accompanied by several members of his family who are known as Barajaatri. Generally the bride's side sends a vehicle along with a couple of male members of the family to escort the groom and the Barajaatri. The groom and the Barajaatri are met at the gate of the wedding venue by the bride's family. A traditional art of the groom is done by either the mother-in-law or a senior female member of the family. A tilak (religious forehead spot) of vermillion paste and unbroken rice is applied on the groom's forehead. His feet are then washed with tender coconut water and he is fed a concoction of curd, ghee, sugar and honey. He is then welcomed inside along with his companions.

Baadua Pani Gadhua is wedding day rituals. As the groom enters, the bride is informed of his arrival by the female relatives. She is then taken for a ceremonial bath that is known as Baadua Pani Gadhua.

Kanyadaan is wedding day rituals. Kanyadaan ritual marks the very first ritual of a Hindu wedding. The groom arrives at the wedding stage, shortly after which the bride is also brought in. The father of the bride then gives the bride away to the groom whereby he requests him to take good care of his daughter. He urges the groom to treat his daughter with love, respect and loyalty that lasts a lifetime. The groom accepts this responsibility and pledges his intention to do so.

Hatha Granthi Fita is a wedding day ritual. The bride's father places her right hand on that of the groom. A garland of mango leaves is placed around their joined hands. Mango leaves are revered for their symmetry and are considered holy in Hindu religious rites. The groom accepts the bride's hands and utters his intentions of keeping her happy and loved always. This ritual is known as Hatha Granthi Fita, the Oriya variation of the Panigrahana ritual. This marks the transition of the bride from the role of a daughter to that of a wife and daughter-in-law. The ritualistic fire is lit after the Hatha Granthi ritual is completed. The couple makes seven rounds of the fire together by holding hands. These seven rounds symbolize seven sacred promises of a marriage.

Saptapadi wedding day rituals where seven mounds of rice are then placed on the ground, which are then sanctified by the priest. These seven mounds represent the seven hills or saptakil parwatas. These are symbolic representation of all the hardships the bride has to face during her married life. The bride decimates these mounds of rice with her right foot aided by the groom. In doing so they take seven steps together that marks the symbolic beginning of their journey together. This ritual is known as Saptapadi.

Lajahoma wedding day rituals is when the brother of the bride puts Khai or Laja, a type of pupped rice on the brides cupped hands. The groom puts his hands under the bride's hands and together they offer the puffed rice into the sacred fire. This ritual is known as Lajahoma or Khaipoda. This offering is supposed to appease the Fire God who in turn will shower his blessing to the couple.

Sala Bidha is awedding day ritual. The brother of the bride, referred to as Sala in Oriya, punches the groom lightly on the back during the ritual of Sala Bidha. This punch is supposed to remind the groom of his duties towards the bride and that he is answerable to his brother-in-law.

Sindoor Daan is wedding day rituals. The bride and groom rise up from the wedding stage, go outside to view the Pole Star. After viewing the Polaris, the groom applies vermillion powder to the bride's hair parting and slips on conch shell bangles on her hands. The wedding is considered to be complete after this ritual.

Kaduri Khela is post wedding rituals when wedding ceremonies are over, the couple is seated in a room and made to play games to make them relax. They play with small, white, shiny shells called kaduri and the ritual is literally known as Kaduri Khela. The groom holds them in his closed fist and the bride will try to pry them open. The same is repeated with the bride holding the shells in her fist and groom trying to retrieve them.

Sasu Dahi-Pakhala Khia ispost wedding ritual ceremony after the Kaduri Khela ritual is over, the groom is invited over by his mother-in-law to have some food. According to traditions, he has to sit on the lap of his mother-in-law as she feeds him Pakhala or cooked rice soaked in water with curd along with Baigan poda (mashed grilled eggplants with spices).

Bahunais post wedding rituals when the bride prepares to leave her parental home, her mother sings 'Bahuna' songs which describes the pains that she has had to endure to give birth and bring up her daughter. Other female relatives also join her in her lament.

Gruhaprabesha is post wedding rituals the day when bride reaches her husband's home and is given a warm welcome by her mother-in-law. She is treated as the incarnate of Goddess Laxmi who is to spread joy and prosperity as represented by overturning a pot of rice placed on the threshold with her right foot.

ChauthiBasara Raati is post wedding rituals of the fourth day of the wedding, a puja is performed at the groom's house where a coconut is roasted. The couple's room is decorated with fragrant flowers and a glowing oil lamp is placed beside the bed. The couple is fed charu or the roasted coconut. The groom proceeds to the room and the bride follows him with a glass of kesara dudha or saffron infused milk. The couple spends their first night together as husband and wife. As per Oriya traditions, the marriage is considered complete only after consummation.

Asta Mangala is post wedding rituals the eighth day of the wedding, the bride and the groom visits the bride's paternal home where they are generally welcomed with a grand feast. The couple spends the night together at the bride's paternal home. This marks the end of all wedding rituals in Oriya traditions.

15. Henna on Bride

Pretty wedding hands

The English name "henna" comes from the Arabic term (al-henna). “Mehndi” is the Indian word for “henna,” and “henna” is the Arabic word for “mehndi.” The name henna also refers to the dye prepared from the henna plant and the art of temporary tattooing from those dyes. Henna has been used for centuries to dye skin, hair, and fingernails, as well as fabrics including silk, wool, and leather. Henna finds its place in many traditions in India. Its application has been deeply associated with sentiments of general public. Even God & Goddesses of Hindu Religion are seen in pictures adorning henna designs on their hands.

Henna symbolizes positive spirits and good luck. Indian Wedding tradition calls for a Mehndi ceremony to be held the night before the wedding as a way of wishing the bride good health and prosperity as she makes her journey on to marriage.

While the form of body adornment dates back a cool 5,000 years, it's generally used today to express luck and happiness, and is often featured at ceremonial events like weddings.

If you attend a traditional Indian wedding, henna will almost always be a part of the celebration. Customarily, only women-on both sides of the aisle-attend: mothers, bridesmaids, future sisters-in-law, and other close family members and friends. A large wedding could see 75 to 150 women attend a Henna ritual.

Meanings include good health, fertility, wisdom, protection and spiritual enlightenment. The most popular traditional use is tied closely with weddings and bridal preparation and these designs tend to be the most ornate.Henna ceremony usually celebrated a few days before the wedding with close women friends and family.Henna placed on the top of the hands can be suggestive of protection and often includes shield designs.The feet are truly a spiritual place to henna, as they connect the body, mind and spirit with the earth.

The core significance of applying Mehndi is to utilize its natural medicinal herbal remedies, cooling the body and relieving the Bride of any stress before her big day.Henna night ritual planned two to three days before your wedding. It takes about 48 hours for Mehndi to reach its peak color. Henna tattoos are believed to provide blessings, joy, and luck, but more importantly, it also enhances a bride's look.

Basically no Indian bride get married without wearing colorfully designed. Henna is applied on hands and also feet. Indian Brides are very much fond of Henna application on their hands add grace and glamour to wedding by hiring expensive Henna designers as it Henna tattoos symbolize joy, beauty and prosperity for bride. Given that the purpose of henna at a wedding is to symbolize the love this couple has. In this chapter a reader can discover beautiful henna design for bride for wedding. Each design has meaning for bride.

Bride pretty hands with Henna

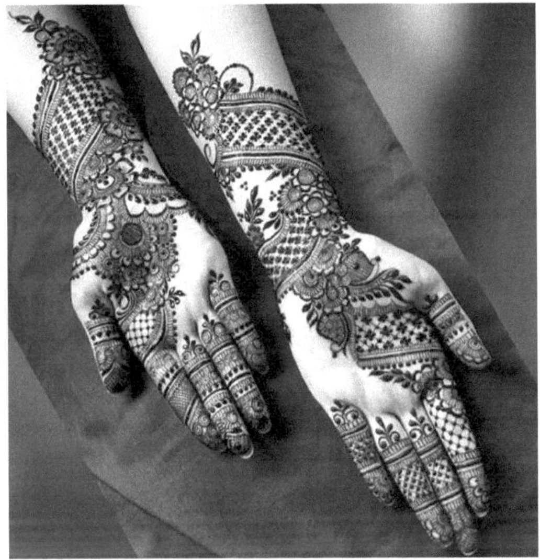

Bride's love, passion for Henna

Bride and henna perfect blend of beauty of grace

Wedding pride with Henna

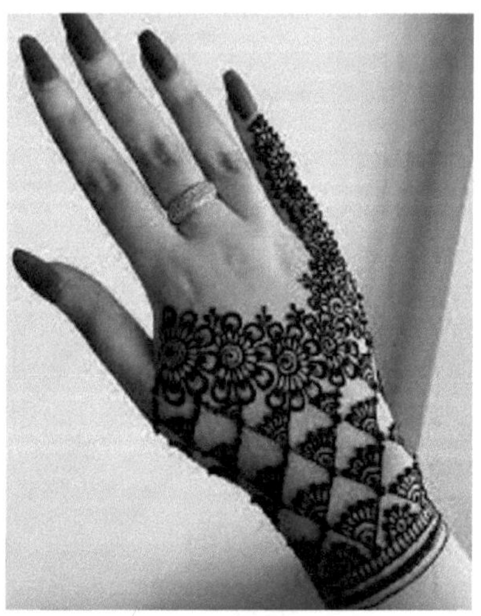

Wonder hands of Bride with Henna

Bride best choice of Henna

Wedding Henna Marvel Hand

Bride's Front Floral Henna

Henna amazing design on bride hand

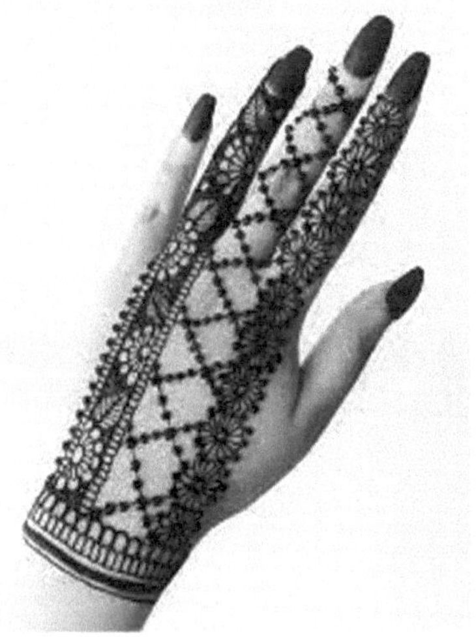

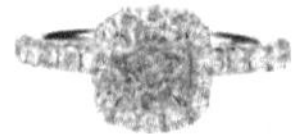

16. Ring Ceremony

Rings are exchanged between the bride and the bridegroom during engagement to seal the union of the two individuals as well as their families. This function takes place only post the Roka (Choosing) ceremony and can be held either days, or even months, before the actual wedding date.

This is the official asking of the bride's hand by the bridegroom's family and an extremely important marker in the wedding journey. Typically, this event takes place a few days, or even months, before the wedding and marks the beginning of the wedding preparations. The engagement ceremony here is referred to as the Sagai (engagement). It also refers to the period of engagement prior to the actual wedding. On the day of the engagement the groom and his close relatives visit the bride's home and present a ring to the bride.

This is a tradition that was adopted in India much later and is not essential to Indian wedding customs and rituals. However, many couples have now adopted this culture and wear engagement rings as a sign of their marriage.

Traditionally, engagement involved both the families exchanging gifts like groom's jewellery, bride's wedding attire, giftfor the immediate family and for the deities. Exchanging rings during this ceremony is a western wedding tradition that we have adopted.

The difference between an engagement ring and wedding ring is that an engagement ring is given at a proposal or when a couple decides to get married. A wedding ring is exchanged at the wedding ceremony and represents the official bond of marriage.After marriage the wedding ring is worn on the hand on which it had been placed during the ceremony. By wearing rings on their fourth fingers, married spouses symbolically declare their life-long love for and fidelity to each other.

After you've exchanged vows, your officiant will begin the ring exchange. They might say something like, “Wear these rings as a reminder of the vows you have just taken.” They will then instruct the bride and groom to place the ring on their partner's finger and repeat the ring exchange promises after them.

Traditionally, the groom will go first when it comes to exchanging rings. That doesn't have to be the case though. Feel free to choose the order that works best for you as a couple.

Then there are the wedding readings and vow exchange. After that, a brief prayer is done over the wedding rings then the rings are exchanged. Once the couple has their wedding rings on, the officiant pronounces them newlyweds, and they are encouraged to share their first kiss as a married couple.

Wedding rings symbolize eternal love and commitment within a relationship. This emblem of love is exchanged between two people on their wedding day and worn to show the world they are married. During the wedding service, the couple will say their vows to each other while exchanging rings.

Ring offered to bride by groom

Getting engaged by ring ceremony

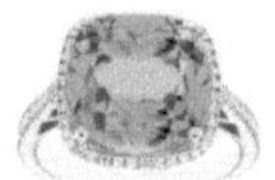

17. Wedding Horses, Elephants and Camels

Traditionally wedding cloths, customized jewellery, decorated horses, bullocks, elephants and camels blend into display of beautiful brides and grooms ready for fabulous weddings full of culture, tradition and custom give more enchanting delightful flavor to wedding rituals, ceremonies and celebrations.

The royal families in their act of royal flamboyance hire elephants, camel sand horses. Elephants are a sacred animal in India, and the union of marriage is also sacred. Elephants represent loyalty, wisdom, and longevity, qualities of a good marriage. Elephants are symbols of good luck and excellent fortune, something every bride and groom need.

Trio the Elephant, Horse and Camel have great meaning in Indian wedding. Elephant is symbol of "Good Luck", "Horse is symbol of Power" and "Camel is Symbol of Love." In Hindu culture, elephants are a symbol of good luck, which is why grooms traditionally ride on them in Indian wedding processions.

In the Shrimali Brahmin community, the girls ride on horses in the same way as the grooms. The significance is that they are equal in the marriage. Horses are a big part of any baraat, whether in the USA or in India. Tradition has it that centuries ago, the groom had to ride a horse for many days and nights in order to reach his bride. It was supposed to be an arduous journey, and a humbling one. This proved he was indeed ready for marriage.

The historical convention of grooms riding horses to fetch the bride is still kind of culture traditionally followed. This apart, horses are even considered as the symbol of power and virtue. This also ascertain symbolic dominance of groom in Indian community who love to practice this custom of riding horse with pride. The groom himself traditionally rides atop a white horse, which is decked out in flowers and embroidered saddle for the occasion.

He carries a ceremonial sword at his side and his favorite nephew or young male cousin (who is usually about 2-8 years old) sits in front of him on the horse.chariot, a light four-wheel horse-drawn ceremonial carriage for wedding is often used in marriages. Camels were decked up with nose pins, ghungroos, and mirror-fitted clothes to make them look fancy for the occasion.

This has brought about a major rediscovery of the age-old tradition of taking out 'baraat'(Wedding) processions on camels to transport the groom and the guests to the bride's home.

Wedding painting of elephant and bride

Bride traditional wedding chariot

Indian fabulous wedding chariot

Bridegroom riding wedding horse to meet his bride

Bridegroom anxious moments of wedding

Groom dressed up and journey to meet second-half

Groom riding wedding elephant to meet his bride

Twin wedding elephants for groom and bride wedding

Wedding decorated camel for groom

Wedding ride decorated camel for groom & bride

Camel wedding chariot for bride

18. Turmeric

Wedding Ceremony

Almost all wedding in India, except some exception, for North-Eastern regions, celebrate turmeric ceremony before weddings. It is most festive filled with fun and frolic. It's the wedding season! Let's take a look at one of the most interesting and vibrant Indian wedding ceremonies, the Haldi ceremony. Almost billion kitchens in India never miss to use turmeric powder to add flavor to their delicious dishes

The Haldi ceremony is a ritual holy bath also known as pithi ceremony, which is one of the pre-wedding ceremonies in India. Turmeric (haldi), oil and water are applied to both the bride and groom by married women on the morning of the wedding. The mixture is believed to bless the couple before the wedding. It is known to have properties that leave the skin fair and glowing. The haldi in some Indian communities is considered auspicious and also signifies protection.

The auspiciousness of this ingredient and its colour brings prosperity to the couple to start off their new life together. In many other cultures, this is also the reason the bride and groom wear yellow clothes on their wedding day. It is known by several names in different regions, like ubtan, mandha and tel baan.

In some families, turmeric is mixed with sandalwood powder and milk while in others, it is mixed with rose water. This ceremony is also accompanied by traditional songs and dances, and in some customs, the bride and groom apply this sacred paste on their unmarried siblings and friends for luck too. It is said that whoever gets touched by this paste will find a good looking partner soon.

Haldi holds an important place in Indian traditions because it also purifies and cleanses the body. After the haldi ceremony, when the paste is rinsed off, it helps to remove dead cells and detoxify the skin. It is proven to be an effective exfoliating agent.

Apart from its beautification property, haldi is also known to alleviate some of the nervousness that the bride and the groom feel before their wedding. *It* is also known to boost immunity and soothe an upset stomach.

Most people believe that haldi has the power to ward off evil spirits from affecting the bride and the groom. This is also a reason why they are not allowed to leave their home after the haldi ceremony, until their wedding mahurat. In some traditions, they also tie a sacred red thread or are presented small amulets for protection against the evil eye.

Just like any other Indian ritual, the Haldi ceremony too is celebrated with laughter, giggles, pomp and colour. This ceremony is done both side of groom and bride and also observed as a spiritual rituals because of its colour.

Turmeric from ancient time play an important role in Indian culinary kitchen dishes, for pharmaceutical local Indian industry and aswell largely observed in India traditional wedding ceremonies. Most of Indian Ayurveda medicine use turmeric in their products.

Nodulose roots of turmeric powder used for wedding

Turmeric grinded powder for wedding

Turmeric(Haldi) ceremony decoration for Haldi ritual

Turmeric celebrative Ceremony

Preparation for turmeric bridal ceremony

Families ladies of bride apply turmeric on body of bride

Bride turmeric application with smile

Turmeric ceremony before wedding bride and groom

Groom's family pasting turmeric, celebration time

Turmeric stage ceremony for bride

19. Bride wedding

Doli, sedan chair

Wedding Doli means pallanquin or specially designed enclosed chair and to be carried by two or four persons, usually brothers and cousins) on shoulders for carrying bride from her home to groom home.

The Doli ceremony is meant to represent the first time a woman moves out of her parents' home, which is no longer synonymous with her wedding.

This is where the bride bids a tearful goodbye to her family. This doli ceremony is saddest part of wedding days, where all days fun, frolic and celebration turn into emotional rituals and one of the saddest part of bride and her own family.

The Doli ceremonies back then were actual goodbyes, because the bride was uncertain when she would be able to see her family again.The bride is expected to experience bittersweet emotion and cry because she's supposed to be sad to leave her parents.

Vidaai (Departure) and Doli ceremony represent marks the departure of the bride from her parental house. As a custom, the bride throws phulian (roasted rice) or puffed rice over her head. The ritual conveys her good wishes for her parents.

A traditionally sad ritual, here the bride says goodbye to her parents, siblings and rest of her family.

Dolifor bride which ranges from a basic canopy supported by bamboo to a highly ornate wooden palanquinis a beautiful way to pay tribute to tradition in your South Asian or Indian Wedding Ceremony. This tradition dates back hundreds of years and it's deeply rooted within Indian and South Asian culture.

This whole ceremony is based on the bride's emotional ties to her parents and her home, and the purpose is to provide closure. It signifies how her life is completely changing as she leaves her home for the first time to move onto the next phase of her life as a married woman.

A wedding "Palki" is similar to wedding "Doli" is a bridal carriage that the bride sits on and is carried to the groom by her brothers and also cousins.

The palki was a traditional mode of travel in the bygone days, a wheel-less human powered means of transport, usually for one person, carried by an even number of bearers, who were known as the beheras.

Palki or Doli also is known popularly as Palanquin or sedan chair for bride broadly used in Indian wedding for brides.

Traditional wedding bride doli

Floral bride wedding doli of modern days

Royal Indian wedding bride doli

Bride coming out from doli at groom home

Traditional bride doli from remote hamlet

20. Traditional

Wedding Bands

No Indian celebration is complete without brass band participation. These brass bands bring thrilling musical and dance experience. In the country of 1.3 billion people, there are at least 700,000 villages. And each village generally has two or three brass bands.

A brass band is a musical ensemble consisting almost entirely of a standard range of brass instruments. The brass family members that are most commonly used in the orchestra include the trumpet, French horn, trombone, and the tuba.

A brass band in traditionally have full complement of 28 players , including percussion consists of a cornet section, a flugelhorn, a tenor horn section, a baritone horn section, a euphonium section, a trombone section including 2 tenors and 1 bass, and a tuba section - often referred to as the basses. A bandmaster is the leader and conductor of a band, usually a concert band, military band, brass band or a marching band.

he Indian wedding band is integral to North Indian wedding processings. While they had a glorious past and graceful, colorful lives.

Traditional Brass band for Indian

Wedding Band for Indian marriage

Brass wedding band of Rajasthan

Wedding bagpiper band from Punjab

Punjabi wedding band hired for day of marriage

Musical instrument used for some Indian weddings

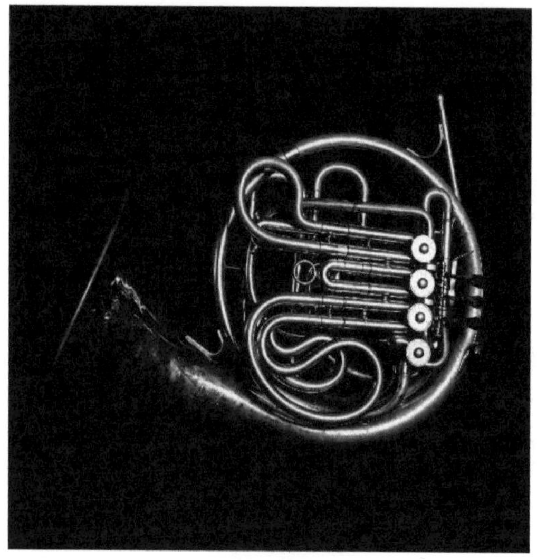

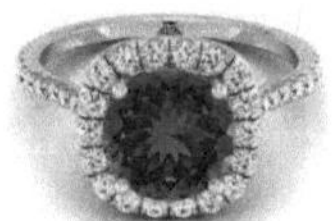

21. Himachal a best

Wedding destination

Himachal Pradesh is the northernmost state of India and shares borders with the union territories of Jammu and Kashmir and Ladakh to the north, and the states of Punjab to the west, Haryana to the southwest, Uttarakhand to the southeast and a very narrow border with Uttar Pradesh to the south.

The region extends from the Shivalik range of mountains. There is a noticeable increase in elevation from west to east and from south (Shiwalik]) to the north (outer Himalayas).

From vast tracts of high-altitude Trans-Himalayan desert to dense green deodar forests, from apple orchards to cultivated terraces, from snow-capped high Himalayan mountain ranges to snow fed lakes and gushing rivers. Himachal is a nature lover's true delight.

Himachal Pradesh is renowned for its scenic beauty, which includes majestic snow-capped mountains, lush green forests, and gushing rivers and streams.

Himachal Pradesh is famous for its beautiful views as well as adventure activities, such as treks, paragliding, skiing and so much more. It is a popular holiday destination with people of all age groups, be it young friends, honeymooners, families and adventurers.

Himachal is well known for its handicrafts. The carpets, leather works, shawls, paintings, metalware and woodwork are worth appreciating. Pashmina shawl is one of the products which is highly in demand not only in Himachal but all over the country. Himachali caps are also famous artwork of its people.

Himachal Pradesh is known for its wonderful scenic beauty. Majestic snow-capped mountains, knows as "Land of snow "is dream destination of nature lovers and attracts tourists from different parts of the world.

Himachal Pradesh is also known for its orchards and rightly deserves the name 'the fruit bowl of India'. The state now produces about 4 lakh tons of fruits every-day, most of them apples, stone fruits and litchis.

Himachal Pradesh is a picture-perfect state that impresses visitors with scenic hill stations, quaint villages, snow-covered mountains, lush valleys, diverse flora and fauna, unblemished nature and abundant trekking trails. It is a veritable haven for nature lovers, adventurers and backpackers.

From vast tracts of high-altitude Trans-Himalayan desert to dense green deodar forests, from apple orchards to cultivated terraces, from snow-capped high Himalayan mountain ranges to snow fed lakes and gushing rivers. Himachal is a nature lover's true delight.Himachal Pradesh is also known as "DEV BHUMI" (land of Deities). There are several water springs enriched with minerals trickling and gushing from mountains and hills. These springs present as place of spirituality as every spring seen by author have ditties of God and Goddess.

Himachal charming destination wedding

Destination Wedding Himachal hill resort

Himachal Destination Wedding

Destination wedding Resort, Shimla

Hill station destination wedding

Destination Wedding Koti Resort

Wedding destination in hills resort

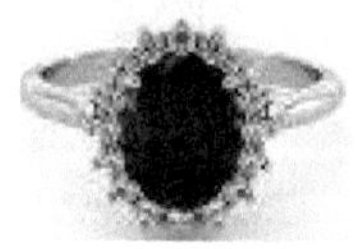

22. Glorious Destination

Wedding Rajasthan

Well, the magnificent palaces, the rich culture and heritage, clear blue skies, serene lakes and royal hospitality sums up the advantages of having Rajasthan as your destination wedding location. After all, planning a wedding in the colorful state of Rajasthan is just like bringing alive your dream comestrue. Hire an expert wedding planner who would help you with all this, if you plan for a wedding in the offseason, the rates might fluctuate. Do not organize a lot of events. Choose your Location Wisely. Take clues from this sangeet ceremony planned amidst a desert in Rajasthan. Hire carefully Bridalmake-up artists. Booking the same property for accommodation and celebration increases the possibility of getting more discounts due to bulk booking. No transportation cost required as well.

Well, this is all we could point to figure out a budget for a destination wedding in Rajasthan. and according to us, your budget should be around INR 30 lakh (42857 USD) to 60 Lakhs (85714 USD)for hosting that perfect budget destination wedding in Rajasthan. A big fat Indian wedding in Rajasthan can go up to INR 2 Crores

(285714UDS) depending upon the kind of luxury you opt for you and your guests.

Rajasthan emerged as the 'Best State' and 'Best Wedding Destination' at the recently declared travel and leisure India's Best Awards 2021. Be it the Pink City (Jaipur), City of Lakes (Udaipur), Blue City (Jodhpur) or the Golden City (Jaisalmer), each and every city of Rajasthan offers a pool of lavish properties to host a picturesque destination wedding and are special in its own way. Rajasthan is not only popular with Indians for a destination wedding, but NRIs and people from all over the world prefer to plan a royal wedding in Rajasthan.

Wishing to get married in the royal style you might know the estimated cost of planning associated with it. Wishing to plan a wedding in Rajasthan costs between the range of INR 30 Lakh (42857 USD) - 80 Lakh (114285 USD) on an average with about 150 people on the guest list. However wishing to plan weddings with 50 people on the guest list, your destination wedding cost will drop.

Destination wedding average cost of organizing depends on a number of factors. Selection of venue since there are a variety of luxury hotels to budget hotels where you can host your nuptials.

Cost also depend on selection of days. It is advised to plan a maximum of 3-day wedding celebration, if you don't wish to increase your wedding budget significantly.

Lesser the guests, better it is to stay within your budget. Destination weddings are supposed to be intimate affairs with just close friends and family in attendance.

Top venues which greatly affect the destination wedding in Rajasthan cost. Samode Palace, Jaipur is an exclusive heritage property in Jaipur, Samode Palace offers picturesque backdrops for hosting a traditional intimate wedding with the best of facilities available with estimated cost of INR 8 Lakhs (11228) which includes the basic wedding decoration like the wedding mandap, entrance decor, venue decor, venue lighting, palace illumination and more.

Fairmont, Jaipur nestled among Aravali hills, Fairmont is a luxury hotel with more than 200 rooms, various banquet halls and a sprawling lawn which makes it a perfect venue for luxurious destination weddings with up to 500 guests. The budget can go from INR 80 Lakhs (114285 USD) to 1 crore (142857 USD) here. Other premium properties where you can consider getting married in Jaipur are Vivanta by Taj, Chomu Palace, Rambagh Palace, Jal Mahal Palace and more.

Umaid Bhawan, Jodhpur is one of the most stunning wedding venues in India. Umaid Bhawan Palace is spread across 26 acres of land and is known for its unmatched opulence and charm. The venue has various indoor and outdoor locations to host functions and can be booked at an estimated cost of INR 2.5 Lakhs(3571 to 4.5 Lakhs (6428 USD) exclusive of accommodation, food and decor.

Other amazing venues for hosting weddings in Jodhpur are ITC Welcome Hotel, Indana Palace, Fort Chanwa Luni, Vivanta by Taj and more. Fall in love with this colorful poolside wedding mehendi (Turmeric) ceremony in Jodhpur.

Oberoi Udaivilas, Udaipur, Oberoi Udaivilas is one of the most luxurious hotels in India which provides stunning views of lake Pichola and Aravali mountains. Wedding at Oberoi Udaivilas costs INR 1.5 crore (214285 USD) to INR

3.5 crore (500,000 USD) inclusive of stays, food and decoration.

Suryagarh Fort, Jaisalmer lies on an outset looking east towards the old city of Jaisalmer and west towards the Thar Desert. Its natural charm provides venues and backdrops straight out of a royal fairy tale. The property comes with 6 wedding venues which include lawns and courtyards that leave you spellbound while planning a dreamy palatial destination wedding in Rajasthan. The average cost of hosting a wedding here is approximately INR 63 Lakhs (900,000 USD) inclusive of food and stay.

Other places in Jaisalmer where you can plan your destination wedding are JW Marriott Resort and Spa, Hotel Rang Mahal, Fort Rajwada and Desert Tulip Hotel and Resort. Destination wedding in Rajasthan cost here at such properties will be between INR 20 Lakhs(28571 USD) to 40 Lakhs(57142 USD).

Arrangements for your guest list to stay at the same property where your functions are scheduled can make your wedding budget go slightly at a higher side. Please note that the approximate cost is taken into account according to 50 guest list. The room tariff at these premium properties vary from INR 40K(489 USD) to INR 55 K(673 USD) per night. 50 people guest list accommodation charges for 2 nights INR 20 Lakhs (28571 USD). Good 3-4 star Hotels and Resorts in Rajasthan range which could be used to stay while having festivities at Palatial locations range from INR 5,000 (61 USD) to INR 12,000 (171 USD) per night. While 5 Star Hotels and Resorts range from INR 12,000 (171 USD) to INR 18,000 (257 USD) per night.

For wedding entertainment purposes in your wedding you can include the local artists to perform folk dance for you and your guests. Ghoomar and kalbeliya are popular dance forms of Rajasthan. Further, including folk music further adds on to the vibes of a perfect Rajasthan destination wedding.

Destination weddings also include transportation and ground arrangements. Photographer and videographer cost. Also cost involve to hire wedding consultant, planner and coordinator. Baraat (Wedding procession)arrangements hiring cost for elephant, camels and Horses. Fire torches, drum players,sand bike, vintage car and other miscellaneous cost.

Also involves professionals like Mehendi (Henna) design on hand, arms and feet. Also arrange make-up artists and hair stylists.

Also have to hire Pandit (Hindu priest) for solemnizing wedding rituals. Bartenders, and more and these service providers could add another INR 15 lakhs(21430 USD) to 30 Lakhs(42857) to the overall budget depending upon what all services you opt for and the quality.

Hiring a professional wedding photographer in Rajasthan for a 2 day event ranges from INR 2.5 Lakhs (3571 USD) lakhs to 10 Lakhs (14285USD).

Pick locations with picturesque backdrops that would help you save on decor. Choose an off-season wedding date. Look out for exciting deals and discounts which are offered during the offseason. Book Accommodation andevents at the same venue.

Groom riding elephant destination wedding

Destination wedding desert dance,traditional song

Wedding dinning place and royal place in Lake

Wedding Venue overlooking lake

Couple celebrating after wedding at royal palace

Royal destination wedding palace hotel in lake

Royal wedding palace for destination wedding

Happy Reading

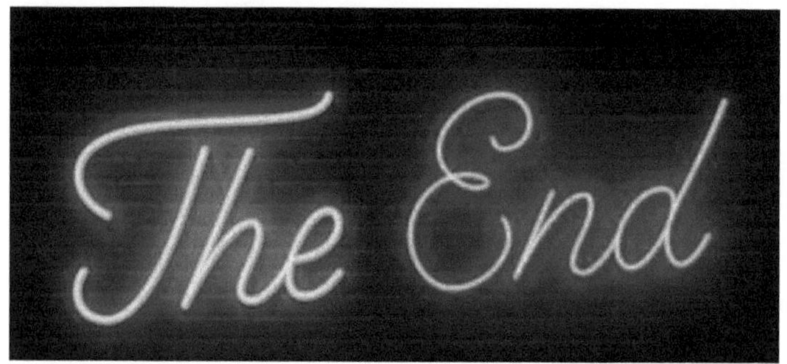

Printed by Libri Plureos GmbH in Hamburg, Germany